Traditional
Sports and Games
of Bangladesh

Raju Mahajan, Esq.

Norah Global Media

Illustrated by Fatima Islam Samira. Art page IG @the_purpleartist.

To request permissions, contact the publisher at https://www.norahmedia.com.

ISBN: 978-1-962957-07-6 (Ebook)
ISBN: 978-1-962957-08-3 (Paperback)
ISBN: 978-1-962957-09-0 (Hardcover)
ISBN: 978-1-962957-10-6 (Audiobook)

Library of Congress Control Number: 2024927407

Norah Global Media, LLC
4520 East West Highway, Suite 700
Bethesda, MD 20814

I grew up in different small towns of the Bagerhat district in southwestern Bangladesh. I dedicate this book to all my childhood friends with whom I played these games. I am grateful to them from the bottom of my heart for an awesome childhood.

Table of Contents

Chapter 3: Indoor Games Played at Home with Babies and Toddlers 79

Introduction

It was during one of those late-night hangouts with friends from Dhaka University way back in 2010. My classmates and I were at our usual meeting place, the Polashi Mor, right between Dhaka University and the Bangladesh University of Engineering and Technology (BUET). As usual, time was flying by over our steaming cups of tea and pleasant chatter when I got the idea of writing this book. So, I casually shared my idea with my friends, and they greeted it with fervent enthusiasm! Their simple act of support that night greatly boosted my desire to turn this idea into a reality.

Now, many years after that fateful night, my dream is finally coming true. While some of the names of my old schoolmates have faded from my memory, I still feel genuinely thankful to each and every one of them. Whenever writing a book, coming up with an idea is always a crucial first step, and they definitely played a significant role in this. I would like to express my heartfelt thanks to all of my colleagues who encouraged and supported me that night.

The book concept began moving forward when I started collecting information about our local games and translating it into English. I am greatly indebted to Kazi Nishat Aunjum (Semonti) for her huge support throughout this whole journey of collecting local games from all around Bangladesh. I also want to express my heartfelt gratitude to Semonti, Fatema Islam Samira, and Abdullah Al Jubayeer for their help with the translations. I would also like to give a special thanks to Fatema Islam Samira for her work on the beautiful illustrations in this book as well as her crucial role in editing and translation. I am eternally grateful to everyone who has supported me in this long-sought dream, both directly and indirectly, inspiring me to turn a mere concept into an actual book and helping to create a written record of these traditions, many of which are beginning to disappear with the changing times.

Lastly, to all my readers who are picking up this book just now, I thank you from the bottom of my heart for choosing to explore the rich culture of Bangladesh through a collection of traditional games and sports. My hope is that you read this book as a journey, not only of uncovering historic pastimes but also of understanding different cultures, in an effort to better love and appreciate the world around us. For me, like all children growing up in Bangladesh, games are more than just entertainment. Regardless of whether we grew up on the busy streets of Dhaka or in the quiet rural villages of the outlying districts, childhood play promotes a spirit of community, celebration, and remembrance that is passed down through the centuries.

This book is divided into three parts—indoor games for smaller spaces, outdoor games for large areas, and competitive games that are more similar to organized sports. Each part is further divided into types of games, with a specific list of games within that section. When you read this book, keep in mind that each game starts with the title in both Bengali and English (where possible) followed by a creative description of how it is set up and played as well as a bit of historical or cultural context. Each game description also includes a sketched drawing or other image to give you a visual idea of how it is played. Some games of the same type are similar enough that an illustration for each is not necessary, but as a minimum, each game type includes an appropriate picture to capture your imagination.

My hope is that you read this book with a curious and open mind—eager to learn something new while stepping into a place and time where the universal language of play unites us all. May this book be a worthwhile read and an inspiration to you.

Raju Mahajan, Esq.

Part I:
Indoor Games

Every culture has its own games and means of entertainment, and Bangladesh is no exception. In fact, some traditional Bangladeshi games have been played for thousands of years and reflect historical events and past ways of life in the region.

There are many fun games that children in both rural villages and more populated cities and towns still play today. Sometimes, when a large outdoor area is not available, indoor/small space games are the perfect option. This section provides a look into a variety of Bangladeshi games that may be played in a home or other building, a backyard, a patio, or other enclosed area.

Chapter 1: Simple Indoor Games Without Props or Toys

Counting Games

1. Aagdoom Baagdoom Khela

This game is somewhat similar to the American game "Duck, Duck, Goose," in which one player, the leader, walks behind the other players seated on the ground in a circle, tapping each one on the head and saying, "Duck," over and over again. Eventually, when the leader thinks they can catch someone off guard, the leader taps that person on the head and says "Goose," and that player must stand and chase the leader around the circle.

To play *Aagdoom Baagdoom*, four or more players sit cross-legged in a circle in an open space of a house, building, or yard. One of the players is named the group captain and initiates the game by tapping on everyone's knees, including their own, while uttering one word at a time from a rhyme. This is what is referred to as "counting." Each player keeps a close eye on the captain's hand as they tap each player's knees so that the captain doesn't miss anyone or make any mistakes. Also, they ensure that their own knees aren't excluded from each round. When a knee is tapped with the last word of the rhyme, the player folds up that leg (see image). Whoever folds both of their legs up first wins, and the last player left with one knee down is the loser. Sometimes, instead of knees, players use their hands and fold up their hands in a similar way.

The rhyme recited during *Aagdoom Baagdoom* is a traditional Bangladeshi rhyme that originated in the Dom Army that once guarded the west frontier of Bengal, giving the game additional charm and historical reference.

2. Chhaadar Khela (Rhyme Game)

Chhaadar Khela is a counting game that is similar to *Aagdoom Baagdoom*. Players sit in a circle on the ground, placing their hands palms down on the ground in front of them. The leader also places one of their hands on the ground and, with the other, goes around touching each hand one by one while reciting the following rhyme:

Ikri Mikri Chaam Chikri (Random nonsense words)

Chaam Kaate Mojoomdar (Mr. Mojoomdar cuts the skin)

Dheye elo daamodar (Daamodar came down!)

Everybody waits for the last word to be uttered. The player who is touched when the last word is spoken closes their hand. The game continues until the last hand is closed.

3. Oobu Doobu Khela

Oobu Doobu is another indoor counting game similar to *Aagdoom Baagdoom* that can easily be played without any special equipment and just a few players. It also doesn't require running around in the sun or any such hard work, so there is no chance of injury either. Any number of players can participate in *Oobu Doobu*, however, the more players there are, the merrier the game becomes.

To begin, players select someone to be the king, who will run the game. The king's role is to touch or "count" everyone's fingers while reciting a rhyme. The king should be able to recite rhymes quickly and accurately, as the game is incomplete without it. All the players sit on the floor in a circle, stretching out their hands and placing them on the ground in front of them; the king sits inside the circle. The king starts reciting the rhyme, and, with every word, counts one finger. The king continues like this for all players.

The rhyme goes something like this; however, it can vary throughout the different regions of Bangladesh:

> *Oobu Doobu dotala bari.* (*Oobu Doobu* two-storied building.)
> *Kaake daake shaari shaari.* (Rows of crows are cawing.)
> *Maago tomaar paaye pori.* (Mother, I beg and kneel before you.)
> *Pootool ene daao khela kori.* (Please give me a doll. I want to play with it.)
> *Pootooler maathay kokra chool.* (The doll has curly hair.)
> *Bedhe debo golaap phool.* (I will put a rose flower in her hair.)
> *golaap phool aayna.* (Oh, rose flower, come to me.)
> *Toke debo goyna.* (I will give you jewelry.)
> *Aami khaabo mishti paan.* (I will eat sweet betel leaf.)
> *Toke debo shookno paan.* (And give you the dry one.)

When the king utters the first word of the rhyme, "*Oobu*," the player whose finger is counted must raise one finger and say the second word, "*Doobu.*" The king continues with the rest of the rhyme and counting fingers. When the king comes to the words "flower" from the sixth line and "betel leaf" from the tenth line, the king pauses, and the finger being counted is folded under by the player, like a fishhook. The king may also participate in the game by counting their own fingers, but players must pay special attention to the king so that they don't cheat.

When all five fingers of a player are folded under, the player moves that hand behind them and keeps it clenched. When both hands are removed, that player gets to leave the circle. The first one to leave the circle is the winner. As the game continues, everyone leaves the circle one by one. The last player remaining in the circle gets teased by the others and sometimes playfully pinched.

If there are a lot of players, it takes a long time to finish the game. The king utters the same rhyme repeatedly, and every player must stay quiet and attentive. If the king makes any mistakes, the players' watchful eyes correct them. However, the king's subtle tricks often lead to quarrels, and sometimes elders need to come and intervene. These quarrels can sometimes dampen the mood among the players, but this situation doesn't last for long.

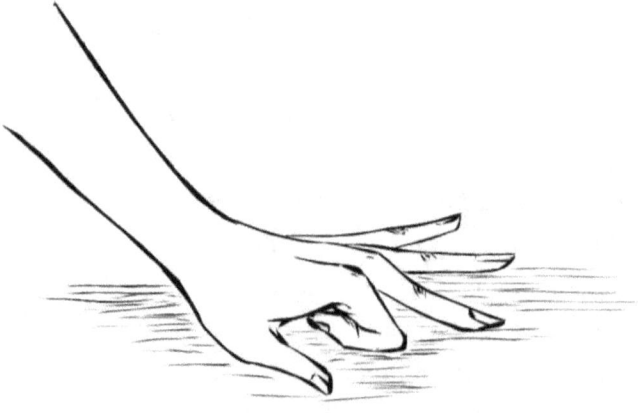

4. Aangool Bhaaja Khela

This game begins similarly to the *Oobu Doobu* game, where one player counts the fingers of others while reciting a rhyme. The finger on which the rhyme ends must be folded under. However, in this case, when all the fingers of someone's hands are folded under, they lose.

As punishment, the losing person becomes the "crow." The other players then ask the crow to bring a leaf for each of them, and the crow goes and collects the leaves. After bringing back the leaves and giving one to each player, the crow is blindfolded. Meanwhile, the other players draw a circle on the ground and hide a small piece of each leaf under rocks placed inside the circle (see image). Each player hides their own leaf. After hiding the leaves, they remove the crow's blindfold. The crow then searches for the leaves, and the player whose leaf is found first becomes the next crow. The punishment of the new crow begins and, as such, the game continues.

Physical Activity Games

5. Chimtikata Khela (Pinching Game)

This game is about endurance, or how long someone can bear the pain of pinching. To begin, ten to fifteen children sit in a circle with their hands outstretched, palms down. One player will choose another player from the circle. They will pinch the skin on the top of the player's hand lightly at first and ask, "*Taan* or *teel?*" The word *taan* means "pull," and the word *teel* comes from the Bangla word *dheel,* meaning "to loosen up." So, if the player answers, "*Taan,*" the pinch on their hand gets stronger.

The player is then asked the same question three to five more times. With each answer of "*Taan,*" the pinch gets harder than before. If they are able to endure until the end of the questioning, the player gets one point. If they can't bear the pain and answer "*Teel,*" the one who is pinching lets go of their hand, and the player loses their turn and doesn't get any points. The player with the most points wins the game. However, if a player says, "*Teel,*" during their very first turn, they lose completely and get dismissed from the game. Sometimes, to win the game (and prove endurance), the players won't ever say "*Teel,*" even if their hands go red in pain.

While playing the game, the one doing the pinching may ask the other player:

"*Kaanda na khela?*" (Are you going to cry or play?)
Then that player responds, "*Kaandao noy khelao noy.*" (I'll neither cry nor play.)
"*Baajarer chera daamra, chere de mor chaamra.*" (Oh boy from the market, let go of my skin.)
Or instead of this, sometimes they ask,
"*Kaanda na gossha?*" (Are you going to cry or be sad?)

The other one replies, *"Kaandao noy, gosshao noy."* (I'll neither cry nor be sad.)

"Chaatro haater daamra, chere de mor chaamra." (Oh boy from the student market, let go of my skin.)

6. Chaari Khela (Ear Pulling Game)

Chaari comes from *chaatai*, a coarse mat made of palm leaves. It is assumed that this game was named so because it is played by making a pile of outstretched hands, similar to how *chaatai* mats are usually kept in piles. The game is for small children.

Five or six children sit on the floor in a circle with their hands in front of them on the ground, palms down. One player holds another's hand down by lightly pinching its back, and the players put their hands on that player's hand one by one, making a pile. Then, they gradually remove their hands from top to bottom.

After that, they recite the following rhyme and gently pull each other's ears, calling the name of the one's ear they are pulling:

Aata Bhai Lota Bhai. (Custard apple brother, plant brother.)
Omooker kaan dhoira taan. (Pull [that person's name] by their ear.)

Instead of the words "that person's name," they insert the relevant player's name.

In Gaibandha, the name of this game is *Jhijhi Jhijhi*. Everyone present pulls each other's ears at the same time and breaks into laughs.

7. Ghoorni Khela (Whirlpool Game)

Ghoorni Khela is a fun game of spinning kids around like a whirlpool after saying a rhyme. Children especially enjoy the hilarious content of the verses. The Bengali word for "whirlpool" is *ghoorni,* so the game is called *Ghoorni Khela*. It is particularly popular in the Jessore district of Bangladesh. It also sometimes goes by the name "*De Paakhal"* from the last line of the rhyme.

In this game, one player is the questioner, who will say the questioning parts of the rhyme. Another player is the answerer, who will say the answering parts of the rhyme. There are also five or six other players who don't speak either of those parts.

To begin, the answerer crouches down on the ground. With each answer, the answerer has to stand up at once, say their part, and crouch down again. When the questioner says the last line of the rhyme, the answerer stays standing after the response. All the other players quickly grab the answerer by the arms and start to spin that player in the air as if the person had gotten caught up in a whirlpool.

The rhyme for this game is as follows:

Questioner: *Teko re!* (Hey, bald head!)

Answerer: *Kee re?* (What is it?)

Questioner: *Kone geili?* (Where did you go?)

Answerer: *Shoshoor baari.* (To my in-laws' house.)

Questioner: *Kee dekhe elee?* (What did you see there?)

Answerer: *Sholer pona.* (Babies of the Snakehead Murrel Fish.)

Questioner: *Dhorleene keno?* (Why didn't you catch them?)

Answerer: *Chaabal kole.* (My son was in my lap.)

Questioner: *Tor chaabaler naam kee?* (What's your son's name?)

Answerer: *Dulal.*

Questioner: *Tor naam kee?* (What's your name?)

Answerer: *Gopal.*

Questioner: *De paakhal!* (Go! Run!)

8. Aanigooni Khela (Spinning Challenge Game)

Aanigooni Khela is a game that also involves spinning; however, unlike *Ghoorni Khela*, the players spin around by themselves in one place, and they compete against each other on how long one can keep rotating. Whoever ends up falling to the ground loses. The last one remaining on their feet or the one who lasts the longest before falling wins.

The losing players have to say this rhyme while lying on the ground:

> *Aanigooni moja bhai.* (Hey, brother! It is fun coming and going.)
> *Dingy aante mone nai!* (But I forgot to bring the dinghy (small boat) back!)
> *Dingy geche bhaissha.* (The dinghy floated away.)
> *Amena boiche haissha.* (Seeing that, Amena keeps laughing while she sits.)

The word *aanigooni* means "coming and going," and the game is named after this initial word of the rhyme. The rhyme talks about a hilarious blunder made by a husband who forgot to bring his boat back, and the boat floated away down the river. Seeing this, his wife Amena laughs. The losing players imply their defeat was a blunder, like the husband in the rhyme, and laugh it off with the fun verse.

As this is a game of competition, saying funny rhymes to make light of losing prevents the players from fighting and, at the same time, lets them enjoy the game and their time together to the fullest.

9. Ektaara Boltu (Game of Leaping Over Someone with Number Rhymes)

This game, popular among teenage girls, resembles the American "Leapfrog" game. It is played mainly in the Barisal district of Bangladesh. The players first choose one girl to be the *kedi*, who gets down on the ground on all fours and arches her back. The word *kedi* means someone who is stuck in a specific place, and in this game, the *kedi* must also stay in her place on the ground.

To score points, the other players must jump over the *kedi* twenty times, without touching her body, while also reciting a rhyme without missing any verses. The rhyme for this game usually contains verses that teach kids about numbers by using amusing analogies. The game is named *Ektaara Boltu* after the first two words of the rhyme. An *ektaara* is a one-stringed drone lute, and *boltu* are metal bolts. *Ektaara* rhymes with *ek* (one), and thus is used to start the numbers rhyme.

The following are some other games similar to this one that require players to jump over another player's body.

10. Shaantalota

Shaantalota is a jumping game like *Ektaara Boltu* where players jump over another crouched-down player while saying a rhyme— only the rules are slightly different, and they say a different rhyme. Also, the one who crouches down is called *chor* (thief) or the person who is "It." In this game, the players who jump support their hands on the back of the *chor* and jump a longer distance in one turn. Their feet can't touch the *chor's* body or fall on the ground before completing the jump, or they will be dismissed from the game. The players who complete 10 to 20 jumps without fail proceed to the following levels, which keep getting more challenging.

In the earlier levels, the *chor* (thief) sits on the ground and stretches their legs, keeping one over the other. As the levels progress, the thief adds one hand and then another, making it higher and harder for the players to jump over them. In the last round, the thief spreads their legs apart, and the other players have to jump over both legs continuously. The one who jumps the longest in this round wins the game. Either the player with the least points or the first player who was dismissed becomes the new thief when the game starts over.

Like *Ektaara Boltu,* this game's name is taken from the first word of the game's rhyme. *Shaantalota* is the local name of a vine-like plant.

The rhyme goes like this:

Shaantalota gaacher paata (Creepers, tree leaves)
Gaa jhim jhim kore (The body shivers)
Jomidarer chelera moorgi choori kore (Sons of the landlord steal chickens)
Ordhek pothe jaiya moorgi kok-kok kore (The chickens start yelling "cock-cock" halfway)

The rhyme parallels the feeling of being extra careful to make perfect jumps in the game. Its content describes the story of a

Jomidar's sons who are trying to steal chickens. Jomidars are wealthy landlords in poor Bangladeshi villages. If their sons are caught stealing, that is extra humiliating, so the rhyme depicts how nerve-racking it is for them. To worsen the situation, the chickens suddenly start yelling midway through, alerting the villagers. Syncing the verses' rhythm with each jump is immensely entertaining.

11. Iching-Biching

Iching-Biching is also another jumping game like the previous ones. The rules are similar to *Shaantalota*, as this game also gets more challenging with every level in a similar way. The only differences are the name for the person who is "It" and the rhyme that is used.

Boori (Granny) is used instead of *chor* (thief) to refer to the person who is "It," and the rhyme has only these two lines:

> *Iching biching chiching chaa* (Nonsense words to rhyme with the following line)
>
> *Projapoti oore jaah* (Oh butterfly! Fly away!)

12. Dheki Khela (Leg Freeing Game)

Dheki Khela is mainly a local game in the Chittagong district of Bangladesh and is commonly played by young boys. It is a game where two players lock legs with a third player's legs, and that player must try to free themselves. The leg-locking technique is quite unique, and it is undoubtedly very hard even for a strong person to free themselves from it.

To make the lock, two players sit face to face with their legs on each other's shoulders, supporting themselves with their arms stretched out behind them on the ground. Then, the third person sits beside them and puts their two legs on top of the legs of the other two. The other two then lower their legs and grab the knees and legs of the third person. The third person must then try and free their legs from the lock of the first two. Although it is really hard to free one's legs from such a lock, this game is a lot of fun for boys, and they enjoy the challenge.

They also recite a poem to add to the fun. The rhyme is usually about a *dheki*—a paddy husking tool used in villages and usually operated by stepping on a pedestal with a foot. This is why the game is named *Dheki Khela*. The game also goes by the name of *Baagh Himshim* (The Tiger Is in Big Trouble), which usually refers to the one who is locked in and has to free themselves.

Before going into the locking position, the players usually fold their *loongis* up above their knees and tie them to prevent them from coming undone. Locally, this way of folding and tying is called *Maalkaacha Maara. Loongi* is a traditional garment worn by Bangladeshi men. It is a type of skirt tied around the lower waist below the navel. It is a very comfortable type of clothing to wear in a hot-climate country like Bangladesh. Usually, it is more popular in rural villages.

Chapter 2: Simple Indoor Games with Props and Toys

Some indoor games require simple props or toys such as cowries, pebbles, or marbles. People may even use other easily available objects to replace the usual tools. What matters most is that the players are having fun, socializing, and developing life skills.

13. Naam-Desh-Phool-Fol-Chobi Khela (Name-Country-Flower-Fruit-Picture Game)

This game requires only a notebook and a pen and can be played by two or more people. The rules of the game are simple. First, a player will randomly say a letter of the alphabet. Then, the other players will write down one name, country, flower, fruit, and picture that all start with that letter. The player who finishes writing down the five words first starts to quickly count out loud from 1 to 50. The other players must complete writing their words before the counting ends.

After the counting is done, everyone stops writing and the lists are examined. Each player receives ten points for each word that starts with the given letter and also has the right spelling, receiving a potential total of 50 points if they could write all five words. However, if any players have matching answers, both of those items must be removed, and neither player gets any points for those words. The player that scores the highest number of points wins.

14. Shoodi-Shoodi Khela (Wear the Ring Game)

Shoodi-Shoodi is a game that pits players against each other to win the king's ring. Players start the game by making the king's ring out of grass. Four to ten players sit in a circle, and one after the other throws the ring high into the air, trying to be the first to catch it and put it on their middle finger. The player who is first to catch the ring and put it on their finger wins.

This player then becomes the *raaja* (king), and they sit outside of the circle while the other players continue to battle it out. The second player to obtain the ring and place it on their ring finger becomes the *shoodi* (money borrower). The *shoodi* then also sits outside the circle, while the remaining two compete. The next one to catch the ring and put it on their index finger becomes the *kotoal* (warden). The one who is left cannot wear a ring on any finger, so they become the *chor* (thief). The *kotoal* grabs the thief's hand and handcuffs them, saying the following rhyme:

Kotoal: *Shoodi shoodi baalli.*

Shoodi: What is it, *kotoalli?*

Kotoal: Which house is the king's?

Shoodi: *Hua hua* house.

The *kotoal* then takes the thief and runs towards the palace. The *kotoal* steps in front of the palace and bellows with their head bowed down.

Kotoal: Your Highness! Are you at home?

King: Yes, I am.

Kotoal: I caught a thief.

King: What thief?

Kotoal: *Gua* thief.

King: What do you want?

Kotoal: I want justice.

King: What justice?

Kotoal: Whatever seems fine.

King: Give him 100 spankings.

Kotoal: How many hot, and how many cold?

King: 50 hot and 50 cold.

The *kotoal* spanks the thief as ordered by the king, and the game ends there. This game is very popular in the Rangpur district.

15. Roomalchoori (Handkerchief Stealing Game)

As the name suggests, this is a fun game that only requires a *roomal* (handkerchief). To play this game, a group of players sit down facing each other in a circle. One player in the group is declared a *chor* (thief), usually picked by a lottery. The thief stands and walks around behind the circle with a handkerchief in hand and tries to sneakily place it behind a player while everyone pays close attention. The challenge for the thief is to place the handkerchief on the ground behind a player without them noticing and then quickly walk a complete circle around the group, coming back and touching the back of the person with the handkerchief to dismiss that player from the game. But if that player notices the handkerchief behind them, they can take it and move it behind another person in the group. Immediately, the thief goes to that other player's spot and takes it. The one whose spot is seized becomes the thief and plays the same way, trying to find the opportunity to dismiss another player. Thus, stealing the handkerchief continues until only a few players are left.

This game can also be played a bit differently. While the thief is hiding the handkerchief, everyone has to shut their eyes. After a signal from the thief, everyone opens their eyes and starts looking for it. The one who finds it leaves their spot and chases the thief. The goal is to touch the thief before they can occupy the empty spot. If the thief is touched, they continue to be the thief, but if the thief seizes the spot first, the chaser becomes the thief, and the game continues. This version usually requires a bit larger space as it's more fun in an area large enough for running in circles. That is why it can also be a very enjoyable outdoor game. This game is mainly popular among girls, but teenage boys and younger kids also play it.

16. Chair e Bosha Khela (Sitting in a Chair Game)

This game is very similar to the Western game called "Musical Chairs." Not only the players but also the people watching the game have a lot of fun. This game does not require a specific number of players; however, the more players there are, the longer the game lasts, and the more interesting it can get. The equipment required for this game is readily available as well—only some chairs and a bell are needed. Sometimes, songs are played instead of a bell.

First, the number of players participating has to be determined. Then, the number of chairs placed is one less than the total number of participants. The chairs are arranged in a circle, and the players form another circle in front of the chairs. One person starts the music or rings the bell while facing away from the players so they cannot see the players moving around. The players will move around the circle of chairs as long as the music continues or until the bell is rung again. As soon as the bell rings or the song stops, the players will immediately need to sit in the chairs.

As mentioned earlier, there will always be one less chair than the total number of players. So, as soon as the song stops, there will be one player who can't sit. Whoever fails to sit down in a chair will be dismissed from the game. A chair will then be removed from the circle, and the bell will be rung or the music will begin again. This way, with each round, one player and one chair will be eliminated. The game will continue until only three players and two chairs are left. In the final round, whoever sits first wins the game, and whoever sits in the second chair takes second place.

This game demands high focus. The eyes and ears have to be aware at all times. There is a high possibility of being eliminated if one becomes a little careless. So, everyone has to stay vigilant at all times. This creates tension among the players and makes the game very enjoyable.

17. Chaar Kori/Kaadi Khela (Four Cowries Game)

Cowrie shells were exchanged in ancient times as a form of money when metal coins or paper notes had not yet been invented. After the invention of coins and other kinds of money, cowrie shells (or "cowries") became a popular toy. It is still unknown as to when and how this game originated.

The *Chaar Kori* (Four Cowries) game is usually played widely by young girls. However, people of all ages enjoy playing this game in their leisure time, especially in rural villages. Only four cowries are required to play this game. When tossed in the air or rolled, a cowrie will land either in the up or down position (see images), as it has one flat surface and one rounded surface. Kids usually collect cowries from creeks, rivers, beaches, or sand dunes. However, since cowries are not always available, kids sometimes use objects with one flat surface and a round surface to replace the cowries. For example, they can cut two date seeds down the middle by the long edge to give them a shape similar to cowries.

To play, players sit on the ground in a circle, keeping an open space in the center of the circle. Usually, they need to sit on a plain, flat surface. For example, a paved floor is useful for this game, so the cowries can fall smoothly over the surface. One player in the circle starts the game by holding all four cowries in their hand and then rolling them on the ground. They have to roll the cowries so that they fall close to each other but do not touch or go out of the playing space. Depending on how the cowries fall, a certain number of points is awarded to the player. The players take turns tossing the cowries. At the beginning of the game, the players decide together how many points someone has to earn to win. It may be fifty, one hundred, or two hundred points.

The rules for this game are as follows:

Phase One:
1. It is called a "four" when all four cowries are in the down position at the same time. The game only starts after someone rolls a four. The one who scores the first four gets an extra turn and also starts the game with a total of five points.
2. If three of the cowries land in the down position and one is up, or vice versa, then no point is awarded; the player loses their turn, and the next player plays.
3. A player also loses their turn if two or more of the cowries are touching each other or one or more cowries fall outside the playing space.
4. If two of the cowries are in the down position and two are up, the player can tap one cowrie to fall down with the others in the same position, winning one point. The same can be done to collect another point for the pair in the up position. However, if one or both of the cowries in the pair touch the other pair while tapping them, no points are awarded, and the turn is lost.
5. The most exciting part of this game is when all four cowries fall in the up position, as that means a possible sixteen

points is up for grabs! Each player waits in anticipation to see if a player rolls four up cowries because when that happens, everyone, including the one who rolled, gets a chance to grab the cowries. In this case, each cowrie is worth four points. So, for each cowrie a player can seize, they get four points. It becomes a competition to grab the cowries which usually turns into a fight. However, it's also part of the excitement of the game.

6. A player can continue rolling the cowries until they have a roll without points. So, there is a possibility that a player who can play really well might score the required points before the next player even gets a chance to have a turn.

7. Once a player achieves the required points then that person plays *loghi* while the next player takes their normal turn. The other players can only play *loghi* when they also have reached the winning number of points.

8. The rules for *loghi* are different from the initial part of the game. Let's say Player A earned fifty points and is now playing *loghi*. Player A will toss the four cowries, and another player will pick up one random cowry. From the remaining three cowries, Player A will have to shoot the first cowry with the third, leaving the middle one untouched. If the player successfully does that, then it will be one *loghi*. In this way, ten or twenty *loghi* can be played. Like in the beginning part, the number of points needed to win *loghi* is also agreed upon by all players before the game starts. After earning the target *loghi* points, players will earn first place, second place, and so on, and will leave the game. The remaining players can keep playing until only one person is left; that person becomes the loser.

Phase Two:

In the second phase, a player other than the loser will hide cowries in their hand. The loser will have to guess whether the player has an even or odd number of cowries in their hand. If the loser guesses right, they get the cowries. If they guess wrong, the winner earns as many points as the number of cowries in their hand and also gets to hit the loser on the back the same number of times.

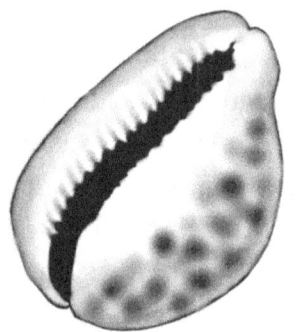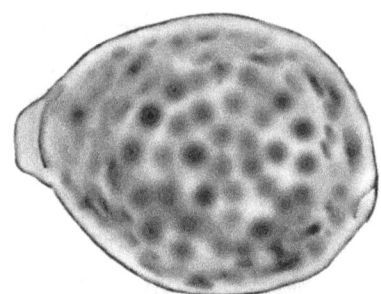

Cowrie positions: The cowrie on the left is up,
and the one on the right is down.

18. Powa Powa Khela (Five Pebbles Game)

This is a very common and popular game that requires an even number of players. The main items needed for the game are five cowries and sixteen game tokens. Since cowries are sometimes hard to collect, jute sticks can be used as an alternative. If using a jute stick, it first needs to be cut into pieces two to three inches long. Then the pieces must be sliced into two equal halves so that they can fall either on the round side or on the flat side, like a cowry. The tokens can be made from whatever is available.

The playing style is a bit similar to the Ludo game (mentioned towards the end of this chapter), and the points are scored similarly to the Four Cowries game. Like in Ludo, four players sit at each of the four corners of a court. Each player has four tokens inside their corner (home) at the beginning of the game. The goal is for the players to get all their tokens to their respective starting squares (home base); whoever does it first wins. Players take turns rolling the cowries.

Scoring points:

1. Five cowries or jute stick pieces are rolled to score points rather than dice. If a cowry falls on its flat surface, one point is awarded. If it falls on its back (the curved surface is touching the ground), no point is awarded.

2. If four cowries fall on their flat surface and one on its back, this is called *powa* (four), and four points are awarded. It is the opening score of the game, so until a player rolls this, the game won't start for that player.

3. If three cowries fall on their flat surfaces and the other two on their backs, it is three points. Likewise, two points can be scored if two fall on their flat surfaces.

4. However, if only one cowry falls on its flat surface, no points will be awarded for that turn, and the player will lose their turn.

5. If all of them fall on their flat surface, it is seven points.

6. If all five cowries fall on their backs, it is ten points, which is the highest point total one can score in this game on a single roll. However, like the Four Cowries game, all other players can claim points by quickly snatching the cowries. For each cowry, two points are awarded.

7. So, players can score zero, two, three, four, seven, or ten points in this game per roll.

Game rules:

1. Each time a player scores a *powa* (four), they may take a token from the house. When all the tokens are removed, they can move a token four cells along the court instead.
2. The players can move their tokens along the court according to the points they score.
3. There is no rule for killing tokens in this game. Whoever can score higher and faster has a better chance to win.
4. One wins the game by advancing all of their tokens around the entire court to their home base.

19. Ghoton/Khootna/Paachkori Khela (Five Pawns Game)

Ghoton is a game mainly popular among rural girls; however, boys also play it. It goes by other names such as *Khootna* and *Paachkori* in the different regions. The playing equipment consists of five pawns (game pieces) made by shaping and smoothing the edges of bricks, stones, or wood. It can be played anywhere with a smooth, flat surface.

Taking the first turn is always exciting for the players. Adolescent girls or young women of the village sit in a circle and play the *Ghoton* game along with the rhythm of the poem made for this game. They throw the pieces up and down with every line of the poem.

The poem goes like this:

O phool O phool O phool dogo
O dogo O dogo O dogo togo
O togo O togo O togo kuire
O kuire O kuire O kuire
Jure ek gutilam jor tulim lothe. (I'm taking all pawns into my collection.)
O lothe O lothe O lothe pete
O pete O pete O pete maathe
O maathe O maathe O maathe maakhon
O maakhon O maakhon O maakhon rongon
O rongon O rongon O rongon bollof
O bollof O bollof O bollof gaach
O gaach tumi boshe pothe, O gaach tumi otho haate. (Oh tree on the ground, come into my hand.)

The rhyme is made up of random words that don't relate to the game. But each line here represents the different levels of the game, with the repeating words being the levels' names: *Phool* (flower), *Dogo* (small), *Togo* (large), *Kuire* (lazy), *Lothe* (collection), *Pete* (stomach), *Maathe* (field), *Makhon* (butter), *Rongon* (jungle geranium flower), *Bollof* (lover), and *Gaach* (tree). Another level, the final level, is called *Haathprishtha* (hand page). There are a total of twelve levels.

The game rules:

1. To start, five pawns are thrown on the ground so that they are not touching each other but are not too far away either.
2. First-level, Phool: While saying the first line, a player will randomly take one pawn from the ground.
3. Second-level, Dogo: While saying the second line, the player tosses the pawn in the air. While in the air, the player picks up another pawn from the ground and catches the first one simultaneously.
4. Third-level, Togo: The player says the third line and throws up one pawn, keeping the other in their hand. Then, they pick up two more pawns from the ground.
5. Fourth-level, Kuire: The player says the fourth line and similarly picks up the last piece from the ground. They finish this move by reciting the last line, indicating that they have all of them in their collection.
6. Fifth-level, Lothe: All five pieces are thrown on the ground while saying the fifth line.
7. For levels six to ten, levels one to five are repeated but using lines six to ten of the rhyme.
8. If the player accidentally drops any pieces while playing from levels one to nine, the turn goes to the next player. The first player may resume the game from the last level they played when it's their turn again. However, if the drop happens during the tenth level, they will have to start again from level one, which makes the tenth level very challenging. The other players also remind the current player about the difficulty of the game by saying "*Bollof paach phool*" (*Bollof* five flowers). This saying means that the player has either all the pawns or nothing.
9. If a player manages to proceed to the eleventh level, the required moves become much more difficult. The player must throw all the pieces on the ground, pick up two, throw

them up in the air, pick up the rest from the ground, and catch the two simultaneously. Immediately after this, they must toss up one from the lot again and catch it with the other four in hand without dropping any. If they lose, they can resume the game from this level on their next turn, unlike in level ten.

10. In the final level, the player must throw all five pawns up and catch them on the back of their hand without dropping them. Since the hand needs to be placed very flat and palm down in this level, the level is called *Haathprishtha* (hand page), as the hand looks like a flat page. The one who wins this level first becomes the first to leave the circle. The others keep playing until only one is left. This person becomes the loser, and everyone else teases them by saying *"Ghaar kheye baari jaay, bang pora diye bhaat khay!"* (You lost terribly! Now, go back home and eat rice with a burnt frog!)

Another game, *Paachgooti,* has similar rules but different rhymes and names for the levels.

20. Baaghbondi Khela (Capturing the Tiger Game)

Baaghbondi is a checkers or chess-like board game, pitting goats against tigers. The playing board is square-shaped, divided into sixteen similar-sized squares, and is usually drawn on the ground. Twenty game pieces, called *bokri* (goats), are arranged in groups of five at four different locations on the board. Two larger pieces, called *baagh* (tigers), are positioned in two random places on the board. Two players play this game, one taking the side of the tigers and the other the side of the goats. The goats attempt to obstruct the tigers' path by not allowing them to occupy two empty spots consecutively, preventing them from moving forward or leaping over another piece.

If the tiger leaps over a goat to the next open spot, the goat gets eaten and is removed from the board. The player on the side of the tigers wins if the tigers manage to kill every goat. On the other hand, if the player on the side of the goats uses the goats to completely block the tigers from moving, then they win. This game is similar to chess, as it involves both self-defense and attack. While chess has war tactics, this game has hunting tactics. Since this game is about capturing tigers in their tracks, it was named *Baaghbondi* (Capturing the Tiger). However, this game goes by the name of *Baagh Bokri* (Tiger Goat) in the Rajshahi district.

In some regions of Bangladesh, people live in constant fear of being attacked by tigers. However, over time, people have come up with many strategies to protect themselves from this formidable danger. Experts say that the *Baaghbondi* game originated from this practice.

21. Chokka Khela (Sixes (Dice) Game)

This is a two-player game similar to *Baaghbondi* where players can eat each other's game pieces in the same way a tiger in the *Baaghbondi* game eats a goat. In this game, however, both players have the same number of game pieces and decide their move by rolling a die. In Bengali, a die is referred to as *chokka* (six), and from that came the name of the game, *Chokka Khela*.

22. Shaatkhola (Seven Holes)

Shaatkhola is a competitive game of strategy between two players. Each participant has seven small holes in two lines that run parallel to each other (see image). The players put seven different small items like dates, marbles, turmeric seeds, etc. into each of their holes

To play, the first player takes the seven items out of one of their holes (leaving it empty) and starts putting one item into each of the holes in both rows in order, either clockwise or counterclockwise. Once finished, the player does the same with the next hole, taking out all seven items and leaving the hole empty. This continues with the third hole in the row.

If the last item happens to be placed in a hole that is next to an empty hole, the participant will get all the items next to that empty hole. But if, during the distribution, two adjacent holes become empty, the player loses their turn. Then, the other participant starts their game and follows the same steps. To win, players have to come up with a good strategy to empty the holes in a way that two adjacent holes will not end up empty when the last item has been placed.

23. Daabba Khela (Box Game)

Daabba is a synonym for the Bengali word *bighot*, meaning "span," from which the game's name originates. This game is played by drawing a box-shaped court on the ground. The arm of the square shape is measured by span (1 span=9 inches). Each arm is about 3 to 5 spans or 27 to 45 inches long. After drawing the square on a flat surface, the angles are connected by drawing two lines. At the four corners of the square-shaped court, the pawns of four players are placed. Each player has four pawns, and to differentiate their respective pawns, they are made of different sizes, colors, etc. Each player can move their pawns after scoring using a set of five pebbles.

The rules of scoring with the five pebbles:
1. The player, when it's their turn, throws the five pebbles high up and tries to catch them all simultaneously. If they manage to catch all of the five pebbles together, then they can take out one pawn from their square and move it from the starting point of one square arm to its endpoint.
2. If they catch only four, their pawn moves up four spans or 36 inches on the square arm.
3. Similarly, the pawn moves up two spans (18 inches) or one span (9 inches) for catching two or one pebble, respectively.
4. However, catching three pebbles is bad luck. If this happens, the player doesn't get to move at all and loses their turn to the next player.
5. The winner is the one who can bring their pawns to the place marked with a cross (the endpoint) inside the square diagram first.

24. Akkelbondi Khela (Nine Pawns Game)

This game is played with nine pawns or game pieces. A court (gameboard) is drawn on the ground with ten cells and five corners. This game may be played by a single player as it doesn't necessarily require an opponent. At first, all the pawns are off the board, and the player places the pawns one by one on the cells. The rule is that a pawn must be placed on a line, skipping one cell. The first cell, occupied by a pawn, can't be used for another pawn the next time. The challenge is to find a strategy to place all the pawns in a certain way, following the rules.

25. Sholo Gooti (Sixteen Pieces Game)

This game originally came from Sri Lanka with the name "Sixteen Soldiers" and later became known in India as "Cows and Leopards." A variant is played in Bangladesh by the name of *Sholo Gooti* or also *Mogholpaathan* (Droughts). It is similar to chess but with simpler rules. Unlike chess, all the *Sholo Gooti* pieces look alike and have the same moving rules. In Bangladesh, village children draw the game court on the ground and use stones, shirt buttons, sticks, or other small objects as *gooti* (pawns). A court with either 56 or 64 cells or spaces has to be drawn either on the ground or on a flat table (see image). Two players can participate in this game. Each player has 16 game pieces, which have to be arranged on the court on both sides. The rules of this game are as follows:

1. Both players take turns alternatively.
2. A player can only use one of their pieces per turn, and they can only move or capture one piece at a time.
3. A piece may occupy any open space along a line.

4. Each piece can go only one cell or space at a time in any direction: front, back, left, right, or diagonally, if that space is empty.

5. If a piece is immediately in front of the opponent's piece, then that piece cannot move forward. However, if there is vacant space right behind it, then that piece can jump over the opponent's piece and capture it. The leap must follow the pattern on the board and be in a straight line. If, after capturing one piece, another one of the opponent's pieces is in a cell next to, behind, in front of, or diagonally from the previously empty space (with an empty space behind them), then the player can keep jumping and capturing the opponent's pieces. Similar to jumping in checkers, the turn may continue as long as one is able to keep jumping pieces.

6. The player may also decide not to capture an opponent's piece and continue moving forward on the board to plan their future moves.

7. In the end, whoever manages to either take all of the opposing player's pieces or surround the opponent's pieces so that the opponent can no longer move wins the game.

There is another game called *Chottrish Gooti Khela* (Thirty-Six Pieces Game). This game is similar to the sixteen-piece game. The only difference is that players use thirty-six pieces instead of sixteen.

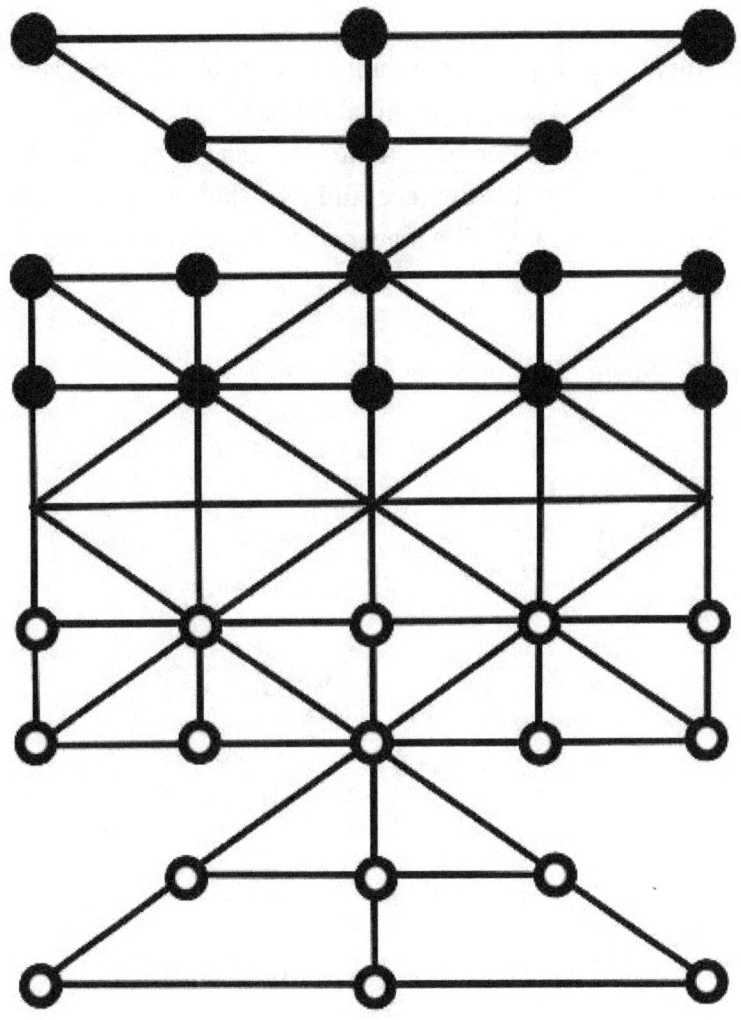

26. Jor Bejor Khela (Odd and Even Game)

This game, which is popular among children and preteens, involves one player hiding a number of small items (seeds, beans, tamarind, or small pieces of clay) in each hand. The person then asks if there is an odd or even number of pieces hidden. Players take turns hiding the pieces and guessing. The player who guesses correctly the most times wins.

27. Paasha Khela (Dice Game)

The Dice Game is one of the most renowned among the ancient games. A symbol of nobility, this game was known as the "Axes Sport" in ancient times when they played with dice-like objects called "axes." They were called axes because, instead of using dots on every side, they had the image of an axe. During the Vedic age (1500-900 BCE), the axes were made of earthen material. In fact, burnt clay axes dating back to that time period have been found in the ruins of Mohenjo-Daro in present-day Pakistan. Ordinary people owned these earthenware types of axes; however, the axes of kings and lords were made of ivory, gold, or silver. But both types of axes were cube-shaped. This game required a boundary or marked ground.

The Dice Game became popular again during the era of Queen Elizabeth. The Queen's dice would always win because allegedly they were cast with magic spells, like fairy tale dice. This game could be played day or night and became immensely popular in Bangladesh as well.

In the Hindu community, this has become a customary game played after a wedding ceremony. After the ceremony, the bride and groom sit on the floor of the house on a new mat. Grandmothers and other relatives surround them. In this ritual, a pot with a narrow opening is brought in and filled with twenty-one cowries and grains of rice. The groom places the pot in the hands of the bride. She tilts the pot and tosses the cowries and rice grains on the floor. It is believed that if the cowries land face-down, then the bride will bear a son, and if they land face-up, the bride will bear a daughter. Then the groom gathers all the cowries and rice grains and places them back in the pot, and the bride throws the pot again. This is done seven times. After this, the bride holds the hand of the groom tightly. The purpose of this is to procure an "exemption of claim." The groom promises the bride many gifts to achieve the exemption of claim. After the ritual of exemption of claim, the bride and groom enter the nuptial chamber.

In the Hindu community, the Dice Game is typically played after a wedding ceremony as well. In this community, it is known as the *Poisha* Game or sometimes the Ring Game or the Cowry Game. In this version, a hole one foot deep and two feet wide is dug in one corner of the yard and filled to the brim with water. The groom hides cowries, coins, or rings in the hole, the bride has to try to find them. After that, the bride hides the same objects, and it is the groom's turn to find them. If the bride wins, she is expected to be a good wife and a fortunate bride. If the groom loses, the grandmothers criticize him. This game is mainly played to check the couple's fate as they start a new chapter of life.

Presently, the Dice Game is only played at wedding ceremonies as a matter of tradition. Otherwise, the game has become mostly obsolete.

In addition to the dice games played after a marriage ceremony, there is another dice game that two or four people can take part in. It is based on winning or losing bets with the help of coats and poles. The four-person version is called *Chaupar,* and the two-person version is called *Rang.*

Three squares are made in the shape of poles or domes of mosques. The dice are thrown in the squares, and whatever number is scored, the players shout it out for everyone to know. Each pole has one, twenty-six, and five dots, respectively. The sum of the dots from opposite sides is seven. The square-shaped "long dice" are around 2.5 inches long each.

The board for this game consists of two pieces of cloth measuring 4.5 inches wide and 6 feet 4.5 inches in length that are sewn together in the shape of an equilateral cross. Twenty-four quadrants are marked on each arm of the cross, and the quadrant at the center of the cross is the *ghor* or "home."

Each side has the last space of the line, and each line has a cross in its fourth space from the center. If the dice passes this point, it's a win. Otherwise, it's a catastrophic loss. In this game, if the dice roll is either six-three-nine, ten-six-sixteen, or twelve-five-seventeen, it is considered advantageous. Mythology has it that Mahavarata gave the example of losing a kingdom in a game of dice.

Dice games with bounds and pillars are not common in Bangladesh these days. Still, some of these games can be seen in small villages where old people still spend their quiet afternoons playing dice games. For example, in Pirozpur, Inderhat, some dice players are still playing it regularly as a hobby. In 2000, while collecting folklore tales, I watched a Dice Game being played in this port city. None of the players were under fifty years of age.

28. Gooli Khela (Marble Game)

Players use marbles or tiny glass balls as the playing pieces in this game, a common game in many countries around the world. Glass marbles were first imported to South Asia during the British regime. Before then, people used small earthen balls. However, the use of earthen balls is not entirely forgotten, as children in some rural areas still use them.

Multiple players can play the game, and everyone brings their own marbles. They first dig a small hole in the ground and then mark a horizontal line (the starting line) usually twelve to fourteen feet away from the hole. The distance between the hole and the starting line is typically less if the players are younger. In that case, another line is drawn closer to the hole, about eight to ten feet from the hole.

To determine who goes first, all players, one by one, throw one marble toward the hole from the starting line. The player whose marble is closest to the hole will get to go first. This player starts the game by collecting marbles from all the other players. Then, from the starting line, the player starts tossing each of the marbles toward the hole, one by one, trying to land them in the hole. The marbles that land in the hole, the player can claim for themselves, and they also receive that many points.

In the next phase, the same player pulls out the claimed marbles from the hole and attempts to use them to strike other marbles lying near the hole, one by one, to get them to fall into the hole. For example, let's say two marbles fall in the hole, and three are near the hole. The player then hits those three marbles with another marble and rolls them into the hole. The player must use the index finger of one hand to flick the marble, like a slingshot. The player gets three attempts. If the player manages to put one marble in the hole during those three chances, then they receive a total of three points, one for each marble they got in the hole. After that, the next player gets a chance to do the same thing.

There are more techniques to win points through hits. For example, a player can target one marble they intend to hit and tell the others beforehand. If the player hits the indicated marble without hitting the others, they will get as many points as there are marbles on the ground. But if they fail to hit the target, they won't get any points and will lose their turn. Also, if they hit any other marbles, they will lose one point for each incorrect marble hit. In another case, the other players can choose a target marble for a player to hit. The play and scoring are similar to the first case. In the end, whoever scores the most points wins.

29. Ekka Dokka or Kitkit (Hopscotch Game)

Ekka Dokka, also known as *Kitkit,* has several variations in the different regions of Bangladesh with slight differences in the gameplay. The local names for this game are *Chiriya* in some areas of North Bengal, *Gooti Khela* in the Rajshahi district, and *Kooth khooth* in the Mymensingh district. Muhammad Abdul Hai, a prominent litterateur, researcher, and linguist in Bangladesh, named the game *Shaat Khela* (Playing the Seven Game). Both boys and girls play this game; however, it is mainly popular among girls.

To play this game, children draw a *ghor* (house), which consists of a series of box-like cells on the ground, by using either hard tools (like stones or tree branches) on soft soil or chalk on a hard floor. The cells are known in order as *Ekka* (first), *Dokka* (second), *Tekka* (third), *Chaukka* (fourth), *Pakka* (fifth), and *Lashthi* (sixth). The cells also have local names; the third is *Chiriya,* the fifth is *Choto Gaang* (small river), and the sixth is *Boro Gaang* (big river). The third to sixth cells are also called *Padma, Irani, Jirani,* and *Koola,* respectively, in the Barisal district. In some regions, the fourth or sixth cell is split into two cells, which are called the "rest" cells. The size of the cells can also differ locally.

A broken round piece of earthen pot is usually the playing marker. Other materials such as stone or round brick may also be used. This marker is mainly referred to as *chaara* and also has other local names such as *gooti* (Rajshahi), *digga* (Dinajpur), *khepla* (Murshidabad), and *chakti* (Mymensingh). The game is played by tossing the marker into successive cells, picking it up, and hopping through each cell.

When a player starts, they throw the marker onto the second square and, skipping the first one, hop to square number two. They repeat this process all the way to square six. All the hopping is done on one foot, except for those squares divided into two and drawn side by side. In that case, the player puts both feet down on the two squares, one foot in each.

The player has to push the marker with the tip of the foot while holding their breath and continuously saying "*kit kit.*" In some regions, people also say "*cchi*" or "*choo.*" They must repeat these words to show that they haven't lost their breath, as the entire move must be made while hopping on one foot and holding their breath. Upon reaching the target cell, players gasp vigorously, and some almost collapse on the ground out of exhaustion when they reach the final cell.

There are rules that can cause a player's turn to end:

1. If the marker lands on a line or goes outside the cell's boundaries.
2. If the marker falls into the wrong cell, not following the correct sequence.
3. If someone fails to finish their turn in one breath.
4. If someone fails to hop on one foot and keep both feet in a cell.

If a player loses their turn, the turn goes to the next player. When it is the first player's turn again, they resume the game from where they last finished. Thus, all players take turns consecutively to proceed to the next phase.

After a player has successfully brought the marker to the sixth cell, the next phase of the game starts for that player. The player will have to stand outside that cell (in some regions, players may stand on the ninth cell). Then, the player throws the marker over their back and tries to land it on a cell behind them without looking. The player will be entitled to the cell where the marker falls properly. In this case, players say they "bought" that cell.

They may continue buying cells in this way, attempting to take all the cells. Whoever manages to take all of them wins the game. However, if they can't land the marker properly in a cell, for example, if it falls outside all the cells or on a line, they lose their turn and the next player goes. On their next turn, they can resume from the cell they occupied last and are also allowed to stand in that cell with both feet. Multiple players can occupy a cell. The opponents will have to skip the winning cell while playing. The game gets more challenging this way. Whoever falls behind will face more difficulty than others, but the challenges are what make the game fun.

30. Ghora Khela (Horse Game)

Ghora Khela requires two teams, each having two players. To begin, two circles are drawn on the ground approximately fifteen to twenty feet away from each other. Usually, the circles are drawn on soft ground using a leaf, paper, or brick or on a hard floor with chalk. One team is chosen by a coin toss. The pair that loses the coin toss goes inside the two circles, with one player in each circle. They kneel on the ground and face away from each other. The two members of the winning team each go into one circle and sit on the shoulders of their opponents, similarly facing away from each other. Then, the team sitting on the shoulders throws coins one by one over their heads, trying to land them in the other circle without looking back. If a coin enters the circle, the teams change positions, and the kneeling team now gets to sit on the first team's shoulders and throw the coins. Thus, the game continues. Each successful throw inside the target is one point for the throwing team. Before starting the game, players agree on how long they will play. Whichever team scores the most points in the specified time frame wins the game.

The name of this game is *Ghora Khela* (Horse Game), as the players get to sit on other players' shoulders as if they were riding a horse. Children in the village usually play this game at home in their backyards.

31. Bora Khela (Catching the Mango Seed Game)

Mango is a prevalent and widely beloved fruit in Bangladesh during the summer, especially in the villages. Most villagers grow mango trees in their yards and enjoy the sweet blessings of summer. Since the people in villages like to come up with creative ways to have fun with regular everyday items, they created this game that only requires a single *aamer bora* (mango seed), which is used after it has been dried in the sun.

Bora Khela is similar to *Ghora Khela* (Horse Game) in that the players throw a mango seed over their heads from a circle. To begin, a single circle is drawn on the ground in the same way as in *Ghora Khela,* and a player stands inside it with a mango seed (only two players can play this game). Then, the player throws it behind them over their head without looking back, and the other player tries to catch it. If the other player manages to catch it, then they get the chance to throw and no points are scored. However, if they don't catch it, the player who threw it scores a point. Also, the one who failed to catch the seed must return it to the circle from wherever it fell. But the challenge is that they have to return the seed by kicking it, and they will only get three chances to kick it and put it inside the circle. If they fail to do that, then the turn remains with the other player, and they also score another point. The game continues for a specified time frame, and the one with the most points when the time is up wins.

32. Deemer Kooshoom Khela (Egg Yolk Game)

This game is played between two teams with an equal number of players on both teams. Two team leaders are selected randomly before the game starts. These two leaders then select the other players for their teams using a fun way to choose teammates. The players pair up among themselves and select two random names for themselves secretly. Then, they go to the leaders and say the two names, not revealing whose name is whose, and ask the leaders to choose a name. Whichever name the leaders choose, they get the player with that name.

The only item needed to play this game is a flat, broken piece of pottery. Two circles are drawn on the ground, one smaller circle inside a bigger one, resembling a fried egg. A straight line is also drawn some distance from the circles. Players have to stand on the other side of the line and throw a piece of pottery inside the smaller, inner circle (the "egg yolk"). The team to go first is decided by a coin toss. If the team that goes first can land the pottery piece inside the yolk, they may continue to play to win points. If that team fails, then the other team gets a turn.

The team member who throws the pottery piece inside the yolk gives a signal to their teammates who then have to bring the piece back from the circle while holding their breath. If they can bring that piece of pottery back to the other side of the starting line in one breath, their team will get one point. The opposing team stands guard on the outer area of the circle, watching closely. If a player becomes out of breath while bringing the piece back, they can try to touch that player and end their team's turn. After a turn ends, the team that was guarding the area gets a chance to throw, and the team that was trying to score now has to stand guard and try to end the other team's turn. The game continues, changing roles in this manner until one team surpasses the other by winning more points within a specific time or number of turns.

33. Mon Kaarakaari Khela (Snatching the Pebble Game)

This game is popular among boys aged ten to twelve, and there is no fixed number of players. Ten to fifteen players (or even more) can play at one time.

Keeping a distance from the other players, one player throws a *mon* (token), which can be a tiny piece of rock, brick, or something similar. The one who can successfully catch it and return it to the thrower wins the game. So, all players compete hard against each other as soon as the *mon* is in the air. Even if someone manages to catch the *mon*, the game only ends if they can successfully bring it back to the thrower and escape everyone's grasp. The other players don't make it easy for them as they all scuffle and try to snatch the *mon* away to win the game. So, it's a game of tussle and struggle, and players' fists get a great deal of exercise in this game.

34. Ludo Khela (Ludo Game)

Ludo is one of the most common and popular board games in Bangladesh. Because of the huge attraction for this game, there are even many online versions available these days that can be played on social media platforms like Facebook or game apps. The easy rules and competitive nature make it a highly enjoyable game.

The materials required for this game are just a Ludo board, game tokens (people sometimes use other available objects instead), and one die. There are several different types of Ludo games including regular Ludo, *Shaap Ludo* (Snake Ludo), and Map Ludo. Each type is detailed below.

A. Ludo

The Ludo board is square-shaped and divided in the middle by a cross. Each arm of the cross contains three columns of squares with six squares per column (see image). The empty parts in the four corners are the home courts, usually differentiated by the colors red, blue, yellow, and green. In the middle of the cross is the goal or finish area called *pakka* (final house) where the players must move all of their tokens to win. The goal area is connected with each of the corner (home) courts through a similar-colored path.

Ludo can be played by two, three, or four players—each playing against each other individually. However, if there are four players, they can form two teams, each with two players, and the teams can play against each other. Teammates individually take home courts in diagonal positions.

The game rules are slightly different for single and double-player games.

Single-player game rules:

1. Players usually roll the die by shaking it first in a container. A player can only start playing when they roll a six. If any other number than six is rolled on the first try, the turn goes to the next player.
2. After a player rolls a six, they can roll again. This time, they can roll any number; it doesn't have to be a six. They move their tokens along the columns as many squares as the die indicates.
3. For every six they roll, they can take a token out of their home court. So, if a player scores two sixes in a row, they can either take out two tokens from their home court or move their pieces twelve squares on the board.
4. However, if a player gets three sixes in a row, their turn will be declared invalid, and no points can be used for that move.
5. Among the columns on each arm of the cross, the middle column is for entering a *paka* (matured) token into the goal area. After getting a token out of home, a player must move it along the whole board once to make it mature. A token that hasn't moved far after getting out of home is called *kaacha* (raw).

71

6. A player can kill a token (send another player's token home) by rolling a number such that one of their tokens falls on a space with an opponent's token. This is called *gooti khaoa* (token eating) and is very exciting for the players. When a token is killed (sent home), the player has to restart the process of scoring a six to get it out and move it again. That is why it is more frustrating to have a mature token killed than a raw one. So, players become anxious if their token is close to the middle column and other players' tokens are chasing closely them behind. Similarly, opposing players become excited when they are close to killing a mature token and are thrilled when they are successful. Sometimes, token killing leads to fights among the players.

7. Once a player can get a token inside the middle column nearest their home, the token can't be killed anymore. Also, a token can't be killed in the stop/rest cells. Every home's starting cell is a stop/rest cell.

8. After killing a token, that player gets another chance to roll the die. If they roll a number that allows them to kill another token, they can continue with their turn. However, before starting the game, players negotiate the maximum number of times a player can kill a token in a single turn.

9. When a player rolls a number that joins two of their tokens in a single cell, the player has the option to make a *jora* (pair) with the two tokens by rolling an even number. Opposing players can't kill paired tokens without having paired tokens themselves. So if a single token lands on the same space as paired tokens, the player simply puts their single token on top of the pair and then moves past them on the next turn. When a pile is created like that, it becomes a temporary stop/rest cell. However, the disadvantages of a *jora* (pair) are that the player must roll an even number to advance the pair

and the player can't undo the pair unless they land on a stop/rest cell.

10. Whoever moves all four of their tokens into the goal area first, wins.

Team or double-player game rules:

1. All the rules are the same as the single-player game except that points rolled by either partner can be used to advance both players' tokens. For example, if one can't score a six but the other scores two sixes, they can take out a token from each of their homes.

2. Teammates can't kill each other's tokens, so they can both land on the same cell and share it. However, in some regions of Bangladesh, this rule isn't accepted, so teammates have to plan their moves in such a way as to avoid landing on the same cell.

3. A team only wins when all of the teammates' tokens reach the final house.

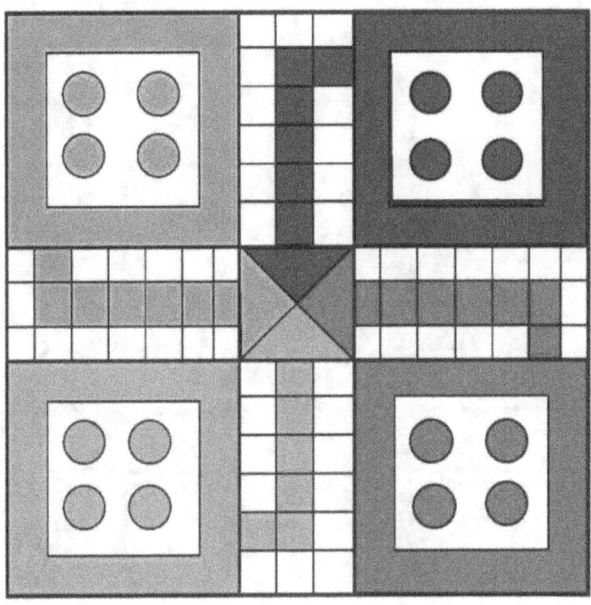

B. Shaap Ludo (Snake Ludo)

Snake Ludo is completely different than the regular Ludo game, with the exception that the same tokens and die are used. The board for this game can usually be found on the flip side of the regular Ludo board. So, by buying a single game board, one can enjoy two different games.

Two players play this game using one token each. The game starts when a player rolls a one on the die. After that, they move their tokens according to the number rolled on the next turn. The Snake Ludo board contains cells numbered from 1 to 100; some cells are connected by snakes or ladders (see image). If a player's token falls on a cell with a snake's head, it gets eaten, and then it must go down to the cell with that snake's tail. This sets the player back by several cells. However, when a player's token falls on a cell with the base of a ladder, it can move to the top of the ladder to a higher-numbered cell closer to the goal—the 100th cell. A player who can outrun their opponent by reaching the 100th cell first wins.

C. Map Ludo

A completely different board is used to play this version of the game. Besides being a fun game, Map Ludo also has educational value as it helps increase geographical knowledge. Similar to Snake Ludo, this game starts in the same way and has numbered cells from 1 to 100. However, unlike Snake Ludo, multiple players can play at a time with one token a piece. After many ups and downs, the one who reaches the 100th cell first wins. Specific indications for where the players can move and what they have to do to move are mentioned in detail on the playing board itself.

35. Chorka Khela (Gambling Game)

Chorka Khela is a gambling game similar to Roulette and is played in a casino. The game is more prevalent in rural fairs. This game is played on a wooden frame or a table with paper and a drawing. A wheel with a pointer is made so that, when spun with a finger, the pointer stops on a cell after spinning around for a while. Players use cash to bet on specific cells, trying to guess where the pointer will land. No more bets are allowed once the wheel/pointer starts spinning. The players who put money on the cell where the pointer stops get back three to four times the amount they bet. The money placed on other cells goes to the owner or operator of the game.

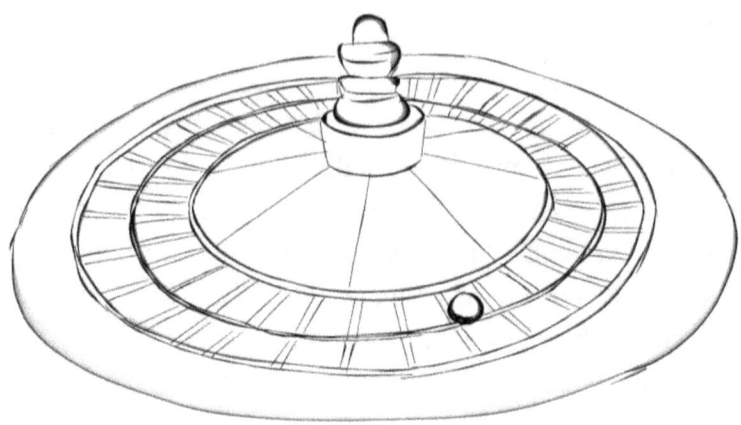

36. Taash Khela (Card Games)

The word *taash* means "cards" throughout South Asia, so a "*taash* game*" refers to any card game played in the region. Card games in Bangladesh use a standard 52-card deck. The suits have a red or black color, and there are four suits: hearts, spades, diamonds, and clubs. Games are played using a point system, and every card suit has a different ranking value. For example, spades is nine, hearts is eight, diamonds is seven, and clubs is six. Individual cards also have values compared to others. Ace has the highest value among all the cards. After that is, respectively, king, queen, ten, nine, eight, and so on, in descending order.

Card games are extremely exciting and relatively modern in Bangladesh. In England, they started in the early 17th century, in 1607 to be precise. By the 18th century, card games had become common in Spain as well.

One of the most popular card games in Bangladesh is called *Haazari*. To understand the gameplay of *Haazari*, players must learn a few terms—Troy/Trial, Color Run, Run, Color, and Pair.

Troy/Trial: Three cards of the same number/face are called a Troy/Trial. For example, one heart, one diamond, and one club all bearing the number two will be one set of Troy. The higher the value of the card, the more powerful the set of Troy. For example, the least powerful is a Troy of twos, and the most powerful is a Troy of aces.

Color Run: Three cards in successive power of the same suit (e.g., heart, spade) are a Color Run. For example, ace, king, and queen of hearts or the numbers six, five, and four of spades. The most powerful set is ace, king, and queen and the least powerful is four, three, and two.

Run: Cards with successive power from different suits are called a Run set. For example, ace (hearts), king (spade), and queen (diamond) cards. The most powerful and the least powerful combos are similar to those of the Color Runs.

Color: Any three cards from one specific suit is called a Color set. Whichever set has more powerful cards in order will be the more powerful set. To determine which set is more powerful, the first (highest) cards in each set are compared. If the first cards are the same, then the next card will be compared, and so forth. For example, if comparing a set of cards from the heart suit consisting of jack, eight, and seven and another set from the spade suite of jack, nine, and three, the latter set would be more powerful as the second card has greater value. The most powerful color set is ace, king, and jack and the least powerful is five, three, and two.

Pair: Two cards of the same rank (for example, two kings) are paired with another card from any rank or suit. When comparing two Pair sets, if both contain like pairs (for example, both have pairs of kings) then the third card is used to determine which set is more powerful. For example, if one Pair set of kings has a five and the other has a three, then the former set is more powerful.

Gameplay

Cards will be shuffled and dealt to four players, thirteen cards to each. Each player will organize their 13 cards in successive value into four sets—3, 3, 3, and 4 cards per set. The one who is seated on the right side of the dealer will start by placing one set of three cards down in front of them. Then the next player lays down another set in front of them. The game will continue in a counterclockwise direction from there on. The successive values of the sets are Troy>Color Run>Run>Color>Pair. The sets of three cards are laid down first and the ones with four cards are laid down last. The player with the highest value set will win one "*pith.*"

All cards from ace to jack are worth ten points, and the rest are worth the number on the card. After each turn, the players are awarded points based on the cards they lay down. Whoever gets to a thousand points first, wins the game. The Bangla word for one thousand is *ek haajar,* which led the game to be called *Haazari* (or *Haajari*) *Khela.*

Chapter 3: Indoor Games Played at Home with Babies and Toddlers

37. Ghooghu Shoi/Jhookoolla Boori (Swinging Babies on Legs Game)

This is a very common game played with infants and toddlers. It is played in many countries around the world and goes by different names such as "Lap Game" and "Bouncing Game." Usually, parents, family members, or caregivers play this game with small children on a bed. The adult will lie down on the bed on their back with their legs bent up. They then put the baby on top of their feet, lift their legs, and slowly pull the baby up and down while they grab onto their legs. The babies really enjoy the swinging motion, and they giggle the whole time.

In Bangladesh, people usually say rhymes with fun phrases while playing this game. In the Barisal district, people use the following rhyme:

Jhookoolla Boori! Kookoolla Boori! (*Boori* means "old woman," but sometimes people call their daughters it affectionately. *Jhookoolla* and *Kookoolla* are just random names.)

Da han dibi? (Can you give me the chopper?)

Daidda korbi kee? (What will you do with the chopper?)

Firi chachpi. (I will make a *peeri*. (a low, wooden seat))

Firidda horbi kee? (What will you do with the *peeri*?)

Bou boshamu. (I will let the bride sit on it.)

Bou kothay? (Where is the bride?)

Jole geche. (She went to the river.)

Jol kothay? (Where is the river?)

Milla geche. (The river is dried up.)

Shonar ghaate porbi na roopar ghaate porbi? (On which wharf will you fall, the golden or the silver?)

O boori tor haaripaatil shora. (Oh, old woman, remove your utensils.)

Dhooppaat. (Sound of something falling, like "thud.")

With every line, they swing the baby up and down. In the end, they stop swinging the baby and ask the last question while the baby is sitting on their knees. But usually, the baby does not understand anything. The swinger then gently throws the child from their feet onto the bed saying, *"Shonar ghaate porli"* (You fell onto the golden wharf) and finishes the rhyme by mimicking the falling sound. Babies love it, and they usually giggle.

In some other regions, different rhymes are used such as this one:

Ghoo! Ghoo! Ghoo! (Mimicking the sound of a dove, which in Bengali is known as a ghooghu.)

Pete foo. (I'm blowing on the belly.)

Kee chele holo? (What child was born?)

Beta chele. (It is a boy.)

Chele koi? (Where is he?)

Maach dhorte geche. (He went fishing.)

Maach koi? (Where is the fish?)

Chile nise. (The hawk took it.)

Chil koi? (Where is the hawk?)

Dal e boshse. (It is sitting on a branch.)

Daal koi? (Where is the branch?)

Poore geche. (It got burnt.)

Chaai maati koi? (Where are the ashes?)

Dhopay nise. (The laundry guy took them.)

Keno nilo? (Why did he take them?)

Kaapor kachte. (To wash the clothes.)

Shonakoore porbi na chaaikoore porbi? (On which pile will you fall, a pile of gold or ash?)

Dho-o-op. (Thud.)

This game is known as *Ghoongi lo Ghoongi Khela* in the Narsingdi district and has two different versions—one that is played similarly to the previous one (with an adult and baby on a bed), and one that is played between siblings, usually an elder sister playing with her baby brother.

In the latter version, the older sister carries her brother on her back, like a horse, and says the following rhyme:

Ghoongi lo Ghoongi! Koi jaash? (*Ghoongi*, oh *ghoongi*, where are you going? Note: *Ghoongi* is another local word for "dove.")

Maamar baari. (To uncle's house.)

Kaere jaash? (Why are you going there?)

Aanbo aatti. (I'll bring my relative.)

Aar kee? (What else?)

Aanbo ghora, deebo dour, Chi-hi-hi. (I'll bring a horse, and it will run saying "*chi-hi-hi.*" Note: *Chi-hi-hi* is the sound a horse makes (neigh).)

At this point, the sister runs a little with her brother on her back, mimicking a horse that is running, which makes the little brother giggle and laugh. Then, she continues:

Ghoongi lo ghoongi! (Dove, oh dove!)

Chirakoot khai. (I'm eating *chirakoot*. Note: *Chirakoot* is flattened rice.)

Chiray kaere dhaan? (Why is there paddy in the *chira*?)

Chool dhoira aan. (Bring the culprit by their hair.)

Chool kaere kaala? (Why is their hair black?)

Naak kattaiya fela. (Cut off their nose.)

Naak kaere lou? (Why are you doing that?)

Sheikh Forider bou. (The culprit is Sheikh Forid's wife.)

Saying this, the sister again runs a little. The little brother giggles and laughs again. She then says:

> *Gaange diye bhaissha jay re aaitta kolar chori.* (Banana rows are floating away down the river.)
> *Aamar bhaire beea koraibaam, jhon jhoinna boori.* (I will marry off my brother to a beautiful girl.)
> *Boorir daate meeshi, Bhai deikkha khooshi.* (The girl has *meeshi* on her teeth. My brother laughs seeing that. Note: *Meeshi* is powdered black charcoal that villagers in Bangladesh use as an alternative to toothpaste.)
> *Chompa phooler gondhe, Bhai naache aanonde.* (My brother dances happily, smelling the sweet smell of the white ginger lily.)

Then the sister runs again and says the last portion of the rhyme:

> *Aamar bhai showdaagor.* (My brother, the merchantman.)
> *Naao baay boraabor.* (He drives the boat excellently.)
> *Aamar bhai baanijje jay laakh laakh taaka pay.* (He goes for business and earns tons of money.)
> *Bou aaibo naiccha.* (His wife goes to him dancing happily.)
> *Bhai dibo haissha.* (My brother will laugh at that.)

After finishing the rhyme, the sister takes her brother off her back, embraces him, and kisses him affectionately. The baby brother may not have understood the rhyme, but he gets the impression he has done something to be proud of and is receiving kisses as a reward. This makes him very happy and excited.

38. Chokher Paatay Phoo Deya Khela (Blowing on Eyes Game)

This is a fun game for building little children's courage. Children stand in a line side by side, and an adult gently blows on their eyes, one by one. The challenge for the kids is to keep their eyes open while they do this. Whoever manages to do this is considered the bravest. The children try their best not to flinch or close their eyes. By playing this game, kids get used to not being easily startled and overcome their fears. It is one of the reasons why the game is so popular among children and adults. Parents play this game with their children both to enjoy their time with them and to train them to be more courageous.

To make it more enjoyable, parents may first say a rhyme and then blow on the toddlers' eyes with the last line. The rhyme goes like this:

> *Teng teng shubari.* (*Teng Teng* betel nut. Note: *Teng* is just a random meaningless word.)

Modhoor baaper kaachari. (Madhu's father's *kaachari*. Note: *Kaachari* is a hut made with tin or hay. It used to be very common in the past.)

Modhoor baaper kheri. (Madhu's father's pile of hay.)

Faal da oothe boori. (The old woman jumps up in fear.)

O boori koi jaash? (Oh lady, where are you going?)

Naatin baarit. (To my granddaughter's home.)

Naatin baarit kaere? (Why are you going there?)

Baagh mohisher dore! (Because I'm scared of tigers and buffalos!)

The rhyme is about a granny who gets startled after hearing rustling in a pile of hay, thinking there might be a tiger or buffalo nearby. She is sitting in a man's house (Madhu's father, in this poem) when she hears the noise and runs away to her granddaughter's home. Although the poem is about a scared woman, children who can keep their eyes open can prove they are not scared like her.

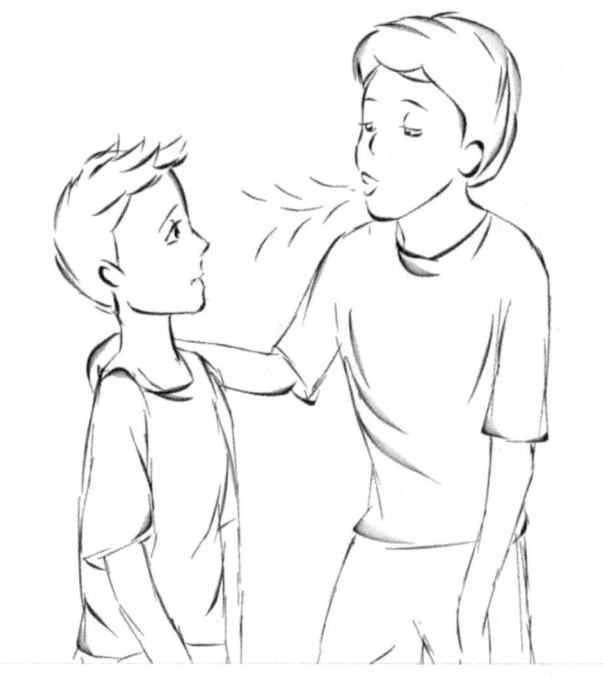

39. Naakataana Khela (Nose Pulling Game)

There is an old belief in Bangladeshi villages that children's noses become flattened as a result of breastfeeding because of the way babies bury their noses in their mother's chest. Since a flat nose was considered ugly, older family members (grandparents) would play a game of gently pulling on the nose of an infant, believing that this would straighten it up. They would lay on their bed with the child and playfully pull the infant's nose while saying a rhyme with an affectionate voice. The babies also enjoy the loving gesture. Sometimes, parents also play this game with their babies. Nowadays, many people play this game with their babies solely to enjoy the time together, irrespective of actually believing the old saying.

The rhyme goes like this:

Aamake ke bole re bocha? (Who says my nose is flat?)

Bhoriya aanbo maati, naak koribo shoja! (I'll bring clay in a pile and make my nose straight!)

Aanbo shingtaar maati, korbo naaker poripaati. (I'll bring *shingtaar* clay and remake my nose. Note: *Shingtaar* clay refers to an exceptionally high-end clay used to make sculptures.)

Some other versions of this rhyme are used in the different regions in Bangladesh. The above version is from the Rajshahi district.

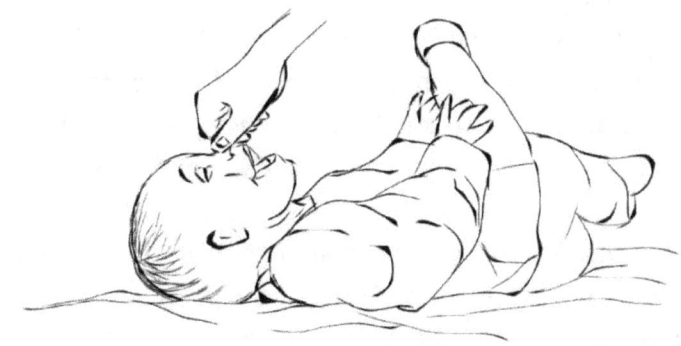

40. Haati-haati-paa-paa Khela (Learning to Walk Game)

Babies usually crawl within seven months and learn to walk from nine months of age and on, although this will vary among children. Some children are late learners, which can become a significant concern for their parents. Parents try different things to help their children learn to walk, and the *Haati-haati-paa-paa* game emerged from this practice.

In this game, an adult or older child holds the baby's hands and says rhymes to encourage the baby to walk. Parents, as well as other family members, play this game with the child. There are also different versions of rhymes for the game depending on who is playing with the child and if the child is a boy or a girl.

If it is a boy, the following rhyme is used:

Aay geda aay! (Come, baby, come!)

Aaitta ooittha aay. (Get up and walk to me.)

Kaauaar thang, bogaar thang. (Crow's leg, egret's leg.)

Naahor baahor aaitta aay. (Walk across the rivers and canals.)

Aay aay kole, khaabi jhaale jhole. (Come in my arms; I'll feed you spicy soup.)

Shonaar baabaa aate! Topon pindaa aate! (My sweet boy is walking! He is walking wearing his beautiful dress!)

Maalkacha diye aate go! Paaloan aamar aate! (My boy is walking with *maalkacha*! My strong boy is walking! Note: *Maalkacha* is a unique way of folding the *loongi* of Bangladeshi men, usually before engaging in hard labor. The term is used here to say that the child is serious about walking).

Aay shonaar baabaa, paanipoori khaiba. (Come, my boy, I'll feed you *paanipoori*. Note: *Paanipoori* is a very tasty traditional food in Bangladesh.)

Gedaar naanaa aiche; Kaachaari ghore boiche. (My baby's grandpa came home; he is sitting in the hut.)

Gedaa aamar aaitta jay; Naanaa aanche jhoori. (My baby is walking to him; Grandpa brought a basket.)

Gedaa kore douraadouri. (My boy is excited and running around.)

Chaabed Aali aate. (My *Chaabed Aali* is walking. Note: *Chaabed Aali* is the boy's name.)

Baape jaibo maathe. (Your dad is going to the field.)

Shaathe jodi jaaibaar chao, taarataari aitta jao! (If you want to tag along, quickly walk to him!)

When it is a girl, the following rhyme is said:

Oi j dashi poddoful Aaitta jay aamar! (There, I see my little lotus flower walking!)

Baindha deemu chool. (I will tie up your hair.)

Oi j dekha jay ghaasher e topa! (There I see a grass flower!)

Aaitta jaiya niya aasho, baindhe deemu khopa. (Go, walk there, and bring it to me. I'll make a bun for you and put it on you.)

Shonaar meye aate! (My lovely girl is walking!)

Biya deemu ghaate. (I'll marry you off to a home on the riverbank.)

Jaaiba toomi aaitta. (You will go there walking.)

Hoshoor tomaar kaitta. (Your father-in-law will be there.)

Sometimes, an elder sister plays this game with her baby brother. In that case, the following rhyme is said:

Aamar bhai aate re shonaar noopoor paay. (My brother is walking with a gold anklet on.)

Haathte haathte bhaitee aamar raajjer door jay! (My little brother is walking, walking to the far kingdom!)

Aamar bhai haate re taapoor toopoor tupur paay. (My little brother is walking with small little steps.)

Ei oothe ei pore dookkho naahi paay. (He often falls and gets up, but it doesn't make him sad.)

Bhai aaibo beraiya, dookkho deeyaam jooraiya. (My brother will return to me after taking his stroll, and I'll make all his sorrow go away.)

Bhai aaibo douraiya, bhaat deemu jooraiya. (My little brother will come running. I'll prepare rice for him.)

Bhai aaibo douraiya, bhaat deemu baariaya. (My little brother will come running. I'll feed him rice.)

Doodh bhaat khaisha dhoom, aaccha koiraa dibo ghoom. (He will eat the rice with milk; Being full, he will sleep soundly.)

Aamar bhai aate, jota aina de. (My little brother is walking; give him his shoes.)

Naaneer baarit jaibo bhai mooja aina de. (He will go to granny's house; give him his socks.)

Chapter 4: Indoor Acting Games and Plays

41. Chor-Poolish Khela (Thief-Cop Game)

This is a game where children enact a scene where a cop has to detect a thief among the players. Four players are required to play the game. Each has to play one of four characters: *chor* (thief), *poolish* (cop), *daaroga* (a sheriff or police captain), and *baabu* (a gentleman, a normal civilian).

To begin, players write the character names on four pieces of paper. They fold the papers multiple times so that the contents are not visible. Then, the papers are shuffled, and each player picks one randomly. No one reveals what character they are except the one who is the *daaroga*. The *daaroga* then asks who the cop is, and the one who received the paper with the cop answers. The *daaroga* then commands the cop to catch the thief, and the cop tries to guess who it is from the facial expressions of the remaining two players. After the thief is captured or the cop fails to guess correctly, the game is played again.

Points are given depending on the character; four points for playing *baabu* and three points for playing *daaroga* are awarded automatically in this game, but the points are not fixed for the other two players. If the cop can identify the thief, the cop earns four points, but they get no points if they fail. Likewise, the thief scores four points if the wrong person is caught and no points if they are caught. The player who earns 100 points first is the winner. The rest will occupy 2nd and 3rd places, and 4th place is the loser. In some cases, children add more "innocent" characters like *baabu* to make the game more challenging for the cop, thus making it more entertaining.

42. Paalki Khela (Palanquin Game)

This is a game where children pretend to carry a palanquin and act out a certain scene. It's played mainly in the Rangpur and Gaibandha districts of Bangladesh.

A palanquin is a large box carried on two horizontal poles by five or six bearers. It used to be a popular mode of personal transportation in ancient times (see image). In Bangladesh, it was a tradition to carry the new bride to her in-law's house in a palanquin. This tradition is still practiced in some villages today. In the Palanquin game, children enjoy imitating the tradition of carrying the bride while creating a dramatic scenario.

Muhammad Habibullah Pathan, a prominent writer in Bangladesh, described this game as follows:

> Children use a banana tree to make a palanquin with the help of adults—or the little ones make it as they wish. Children also make two dolls, one is the bride and the other

is the groom. They place these dolls inside the makeshift palanquin facing each other. Four players acting as the bearers carry it on their shoulders. Sometimes the bearers change their position and recite a poem. Throughout the poem, they say to the passersby to clear the path as they are proceeding with the palanquin, and to make it fun they even add that the bride is really heavy.

While carrying the makeshift palanquin, children pretend as if the path is full of dangerous tigers, snakes, and robbers. If they are careless for even a moment, they might face grave consequences. So, they pretend to step very carefully to avoid these dangers. While acting that out, they warn each other by saying, "Beware of the tigers, snakes, robbers, and thorny paths."

At some point, they pretend that they have faced a certain danger directly, perhaps a tiger or a robber. They act as if they were scared out of their wits and run away to save themselves, leaving the palanquin on the ground. The game finishes there.

43. Paakhi Shikaar Khela (Bird Hunting Game)

This is a fun game where children act like they are hunting baby birds. Some play the role of the hunters, and the rest are the birds. The children draw two courts on the ground, some distance apart. One is a nest, and the other is a cage. A line is drawn in the middle, between the courts. One child plays the role of the mother bird and stands before the nest court, protecting the baby birds. Two children act as hunters, who hop around outside the nest trying to catch the baby birds.

To catch a baby bird, the hunters have to cross the center line, reach the nest, and touch (tag) the children playing baby birds without getting tagged by the mother bird. If they can tag a baby bird, leave the nest, cross the line, and get to the cage court, the baby bird that they tagged will be captured. However, if they get tagged by the mother first, they will lose their prey. Once they are on the side of the line that has the cage, the mother bird can't touch them. Thus, the game continues. If the hunters keep losing their prey, they will be dismissed from the game. If they can dismiss both hunters, the birds win. However, if the hunters manage to capture all the baby birds before getting dismissed, the hunters win.

While playing the game, the kids recite poems. The rhyme that the hunters say is directed at the baby birds, with lines that call them to come to them, alluring them with food and care. The captured birds also use rhymes that say they regret getting captured and it is really unfair to them.

44. Proshnobaachok Khela (Questioning Game)

This game is played between two players using a series of funny, made-up questions and answers. One player asks the questions and the other gives the answers. The answerer purposefully acts a little idiotic, as if they are the victim of an absurd questioning session, to make it funny for the audience. The absurdity and craziness of the remarks about the questions and answers make the other children laugh. This game is popular in the Barisal, Pirojpur, Jhalakathi, and Patuakhali districts.

45. Bang er Maatha Khela (Frog's Head Game)

The Frog's Head Game is another question-and-answer game like the previous one. However, in this game, the questions and answers are in the form of a poem that was created for this game. Also, in this game, it is the questioner who plays the victim to the answerer's absurd remarks. The answerer leads the replies in a way that the questioner has to ask an obvious question and gets ridiculed. This amuses the audience. The rhymes are memorized and presented as such in the game. The Frog's Head Game is common in North Bengal and South Bengal, however, it is most popular in the Rajshahi district.

The game starts with the answerer saying to the questioner in a whimsical tone, "*Ek kotha*" (I have something to say to you).

Questioner: *Kee kotha?* (What is it?)

Answerer: *Bang er maatha.* (Frog's head.)

Questioner: *Kee bang?* (What kind of frog?)

Answerer: *Shoru bang.* (A slender frog.)

Questioner: *Kee shoru?* (How slender?)

Answerer: *Baamon shoru.* (Slender as a dwarf.)

Questioner: *Kee baamon?* (What dwarf?)

94

Answerer: *Haater baamon.* (Dwarf from the market.)

Questioner: *Kee haat?* (Which market?)

Answerer: *Ghora haat.* (Horse-selling market.)

Questioner: *Kee ghora?* (What kind of horse?)

Answerer: *Neel ghora.* (Blue horse.)

Questioner: *Kee neel?* (What kind of blue?)

Answerer: *Aaga dheel.* (The tip is loose.)

Questioner: *Kee aaga?* (Tip of what?)

Answerer: *Boger paakha.* (Crane's wings.)

Questioner: *Kee bok?* (Which crane?)

Answerer: *Kaani bok.* (Blind crane.)

Questioner: *Kee kaani?* (Blind how?)

Answerer: *Dhaan bhaani.* (By husking paddy.)

Questioner: *Kee dhaan?* (Which paddy?)

Answerer: *Fao dhaan.* (Extra paddy.)

Questioner: *Kee fao?* (What was extra?)

Answerer: *Goo khao!* (Eat rubbish!)

The last insulting remark is a trap that the questioner falls into by questioning every reply. The questioner acts flabbergasted at this remark, as if they didn't see it coming. Their reaction entertains the audience, and the game ends here.

46. Raaja Kotoal Khela (Warden of the King Game)

In this game, one child plays the *raaja* (king), one plays the *kotoal* (warden), and all the other players are banana trees. The king sits in a circle with everyone except the warden. Everyone makes a fist and puts it on the king's hand, pretending as if their hands are a stack of banana clusters (see image). The warden moves around the outside of the circle. Then *raaja* and *kotoal* converse with each other through a series of questions and answers.

Their conversation goes like this:

> King: *Kaanootar piche ke ghore?* (Who is loitering behind the boat?)
> Warden: *Raajar Kotoal.* (It's me, the King's Warden.)
> King: *Keesher jonno?* (What for?)
> Warden: *Ek chori kolaar jonno.* (Only for some bananas.)
> King: *Kaal j leea gechile?* (Didn't you take some yesterday?)
> Warden: *Ghorar laad porche.* (The horse dung made them dirty.)
> King: *Dhuiye khaonee?* (Didn't you eat any after washing them?)
> Warden: *Chih chih! Thuh!* (Eww! Eww! Ptui!)
> King: *Tobe ek chori leea jao.* (Then take one stack of bananas with you.)

After hearing the last sentence, the warden takes it as permission from the king and proceeds to mimic cutting off one of the player's two fists as if cutting off a cluster of bananas. The warden takes the bananas, and the player whose hands were cut leaves the circle with the warden. Then the conversation starts again, and the warden proceeds to take all the players away one by one. The children laugh when the warden cuts their hands, and it becomes an entertaining moment for them. When the last stack of bananas has been cut and removed, the game ends. Little children enjoy acting and playing their roles. Sometimes, players change roles to prove their acting is better than the previous player.

47. Ikri-Mikri Khela (Catching the Thief Game)

Ikri Mikri is a fun indoor game of catching a thief among the players. This game is also known as *Ijibiji Khara* in the Chakma tribe of Bangladesh. Like many South Asian games, it is played while reciting a rhyme.

To play, children sit on their knees in a circle and place their hands in front of them on the ground. The oldest child plays the role of leader and recites the verse. The rhyme starts with different words in different regions, such as *Ichan Bichan, Iching Biching, Itkiri Mitkiri*, etc. The leader begins to recite the rhyme and taps the hand of each player, one by one, with every word. On the last word, whoever's hand gets tapped lifts up that hand and presses it to their abdomen or armpit, warming it up. The leader keeps repeating the rhyme and tapping the players' hands until the last player's hand has been warmed. After all players have been covered, the leader checks everyone's hand to see whether it is warm or not. The player who has a cold hand is declared a thief, which is considered an insult. Then, the leader pretends to cut the hands of the thief, using their own hand like a knife, and the thief acts like they are in pain. All the other children laugh at this.

In some regions, players don't warm their hands; they just put their hands in fists behind them. Ashutosh Bhattacharya, a prominent scholar in Bangladesh, described this version, "When all the players with their hands clenched behind them bring both fisted hands in front of them, the leader acts as if he is about to cut everyone's fists one by one with a sword. Then everyone opens their fists by uttering the word *bhooa* (fake) in an exuberant laugh." This laughing means that the players know the one playing the executioner is fake, and they are not afraid to be called a thief. Young children enjoy this playful acting.

Ikri Mikri is named after the first verse of the rhyme. In brief, the rhyme says that it is the king's order to find the thief and cut off their hand in public. The rhyme represents a sense of heroism (the king's power) and insulting remarks to the thief. The first part of *Ikri Mikri* belongs to the "game of chance," becoming a thief by chance. In the end, the game is a reflection of the social norms of the region, as punishing a thief by cutting off their hand is a legal rule of the Islamic state. That practice may have inspired this game.

48. Kothha Khela (Acting out a Robbery Story Game)

The story of catching a robber trying to steal something is acted out during this game, which is really more like a skit. Usually, adolescents play the actors, and children and adults come to see them perform. The skit is usually performed in the evening using a *hazaak* lamp (gas lamp), which gives it a more dramatic ambiance. The name of the game, *Kothha Khela,* comes from the Bangla word *loothi* or *koothi baari*, which is the traditional house for wealthy villagers like the *Jomidaar* (Zamindar, or landlords) and other powerful individuals. The story is described below:

A Zamindar with a *kothha* house has a huge army. In one of the rooms in the house, there are precious gems. His guards, with sticks as weapons, watch over the gem room. One day, a gang of formidable robbers gives the Zamindar a letter saying they will come to rob his house and take all his jewels on a certain date. The landlord then employs an army of soldiers to guard the room day and night. One night, the daring robber gang comes to his house, shouting and announcing their presence from afar. Hearing this, the landlord's army warns the other guards by making various sounds.

Realizing it will not be easy to loot the house due to the large number of guards, the robbers resort to other tactics. The robbers appeal to the chief of the army by promising the chief a part of the loot. The chief then betrays the landlord's trust and lets the gang sneak into the room with the gems. The robbers enter the room and start looting. However, some guards take notice, and a fierce battle breaks out. But the robbers, along with the traitor, overpower most of the loyal guards. Realizing the grave situation and the small odds of fighting off the robbers, some clever guards set traps with mud ropes, and eventually, the robbers get caught.

This story is acted out, scene by scene, like a play. The scenes are given below:

Scene 1: The actors prepare a small stage area for the play, where the scenery and props for the landlord's house and the gem room are set up using readily available items like clothes, paper, etc. Then, many guards with sticks enter the scene. They perform various types of dances to the beat of musical instruments in front of the landlord's house.

Scene 2: The landlord receives the letter from the robber gang and orders an army to guard the gem room.

Scene 3: The army of guards gather around the room to protect it, swinging their sticks.

Scene 4: The robbers arrive and start shouting threatening words in the direction of the house from a distance. Upon hearing them, the guards also start shouting back that they are not afraid. Seeing the size of the battle-prepared army, the robbers start to discuss among themselves in low voices that their war tactics need changing. Then, they devise a plan.

Scene 5: The robbers come in disguise and allure the army chief with a bribe. The greedy chief then lets them know the details about the army and the layout of the mansion. He weakens the defenses near the gem room by sending the guards to patrol elsewhere. Then, he sneakily lets the robbers get into the room. The robbers start looting gems and jewelry.

Scene 6: One of the guards, noticing that something seemed off with the chief's behavior, goes to check on the gem room without the chief noticing and sees the robbers inside. He immediately whistles loudly, signaling all the other guards. They all roar with anger and start to attack the robbers. However, the robbers have the advantage as they know the inside details about the terrain and the guards from the traitor chief. Leaving the loot in the room, they start to fight off the guards, defeating almost all of them one by one.

Scene 7: Seeing imminent defeat, the clever guard schemes a plan with some of the other guards. At first, they hit the traitor chief on the head, knocking him senseless so he can't give away their plan or warn the robbers. Then, they set up a trap with rope at the main entrance of the gem room while the battle continues outside, and they hide near the trap. When the robbers return for the loot after defeating the rest of the army, the clever guards hiding nearby wait for them to walk under the trap and pull the rope. The rope gets tied around the waist of the robbers and they get stuck. The guards come out of their hiding place and start to attack the immobilized robbers. The robbers try to free themselves from the trap and fight back, but in the end, they are defeated.

In this game, the head of the robber gang usually steals the spotlight for his daring plan to attack a powerful landlord and his army head-on. Even when stuck in the trap in the end, he fights until the last moment. Although their society generally disapproves of robbers, in Bangladeshi villages, some landlords were known for cruelty and mercilessly ruling over the poor, powerless villagers. So, daring to attack a landlord's property was seen as an act of bravery and heroism. The gang leader is even rewarded at the end of the game for his fighting skills.

The audience enjoys this performance and gets immersed in the story. Since television and internet weren't always available in some rural areas, this kind of play was a huge attraction for the villagers.

49. Koillya Khela (The Cuckoo Bird Game)

Koillya is the local version of the Bengali word *kokil* (cuckoo bird). This game centers around a cuckoo bird, which is why the game is named *Koillya Khela*. It is played mainly in the Chittagong, Comilla, Tangail, and Barisal districts.

The game can be played with multiple players, usually adolescents, and no specific number of players is required. However, if there are more than five or six players, the game is more fun. One child plays the cuckoo bird, and this person is chosen through a lottery. The other players join hands and make a circle which is a "pond." The player who is the cuckoo bird stands outside the pond and starts crying. Seeing the bird cry, the players in the circle start to ask the bird questions, which the cuckoo answers.

The conversation goes like this:

    Players: *Tor naam kee?* (What's your name?)

    Cuckoo: *Aamar naam Koillya.* (My name is Koilla.)

    Players: *Kaadcho keno?* (Why are you crying?)

    Cuckoo: *Ekti pookoorer jonno kaadchi.* (I'm crying for a pond.)

    Players: *Pookoor deeye kee korbe?* (What would you do with a pond?)

    Cuckoo: *Boda paartam.* (Lay eggs.)

    Players: *Ekhane pookoor dekhchona?* (Can't you see this pond here?)

    Cuckoo: *Etee to choto pookoor.* (But it's a small one.)

    Players: *Taaka deele boro hoye jaabe.* (Money can make it larger.)

Hearing this, the cuckoo bird then throws some toys or stones inside the circle, mimicking giving money to them. Then, the players in the circle all step back to make the circle bigger. The bird tries to move into the pond from under the players' hands. However, whichever way the cuckoo tries to enter, it gets blocked by the players. Then, the players recite a poem about why the cuckoo can't enter wherever it wants.

The poem they say is:

    Edike khonta aache. (There is a shovel here.)

    Edike kooraal aache. (There is an axe here.)

    Edike daa aache. (There is a sickle here.)

    Edike choori aache. (There is a knife here.)

    Edike paaraa aache. (There is a flat stone here.)

    Edike poota aache. (There is a grinder here.)

Basically, the players don't want to let the bird enter the pond, so they make false excuses to not let the bird in. Realizing this, the bird forcibly creates an opening by separating two players holding hands and enters the circle. After the cuckoo enters, the players in the circle begin a new way of bothering the bird.

The interrogation goes like this.

> Players: *Koillya boda perecho kee?* (Koillya, did you lay eggs?)
> Koillya: *Perechi.* (I did.)
> Players: *Koy dol perecho?* (How many?)
> Koillya: *Eksho dol.* (One hundred.)
> Players: *Ghora pooriecho kee?* (Have you filled the jar with eggs?)
> Koillya: *Poorini.* (I haven't filled it.)
> Players: *Goru ghorer gobor felecho kee?* (Have you cleaned the cow dung in the cowhouse?)
> Koillya: *Felini.* (I haven't.)
> Players: *Jaamai ke bhaat diyecho kee?* (Have you fed your spouse rice?)
> Koillya: *Deini.* (I haven't.)
> Players: *Chelemeye der gosol diyecho kee?* (Have you bathed your children?)
> Koillya: *Koraini.* (I haven't.)

The players then remind the cuckoo to leave its eggs in the pond when it goes to do the above-mentioned chores. When the bird leaves, all of them pretend to eat the eggs. After some time, the bird returns, acting as if it has finished all its chores, and it finds all the eggs have been eaten. It gets very sad and angry and starts chasing the players to get its revenge. The players begin running to and fro, and it now becomes a game of tag. Whoever gets caught first becomes the cuckoo bird in the next round, and the game continues.

Koillya Khela is a game that reflects the cruel reality and injustice in society from the children's point of view. The ones having power, especially in villages, often forcibly seize lands or ownership from the powerless. No matter how much the powerless struggle or sometimes even invest their life savings, they don't always get their rightful property back. In the cuckoo bird's story, the bird is sad because it can't lay eggs as there is no pond. The others get the bird to invest money in a bigger pond, but even after it does, they don't let it inside. And when it finally does make its way inside, the others take notice of its eggs, just as greedy people lust over other people's possessions. Then they trick the cuckoo into leaving its valuables behind, and they steal them while it is away. This reflects a very common scenario of injustice in society. Sometimes, the conflict may be resolved by catching the person responsible, as is shown in the game when the bird catches a player. However, not all the culprits get caught in the game. Nevertheless, something is still better than nothing for the victim bird.

50. Teea re Teea Khela (The Parrot Bird Game)

Teea re Teea Khela is a game of one person pretending to be a parrot bird. *Teea* is Bengali for parrot, which is where the game's name comes from. Young boys enjoy this game very much.

To begin, one boy lies with his face on the ground, supporting himself on the palms of his hands. He stretches his legs behind him and lifts them up a little. This way, he pretends to be a *teea paakhi* (parakeet/parrot). The others stand behind him, grab both of his legs, and lift them two to three feet above the ground (see image).

Two boys kneel on the ground on either side of him and put their fists under the bird's abdomen.

After that, a series of questions and answers are recited between the bird and others. The bird is gently slapped on the back while questioning. Each time the parrot replies, the boy playing the bird sways his body a little in the front and then in the back like he is a bird swinging on a tree branch. He responds in a playful manner.

The Q&A session is as follows:

> Players: *Teea re teea!* (*Teea*! Hey, *teea*!)
> The bird: *Keere bhai teea?* (What is it, Brother *teea*?)
> Players: *Tor bou kee raanche?* (What has your wife cooked?)
> The bird: *Begoon vaaja.* (Eggplant fries.)
> Players: *Aamake ektoo deebe?* (Would you give me a little?)
> The bird: *Ekai baarite, bhaangtaam maaja.* (I am alone at home, and my back is breaking down.)

The conversation doesn't really have much meaning, but boys especially enjoy the swinging and acting like a bird. The boys take turns playing the role of the bird.

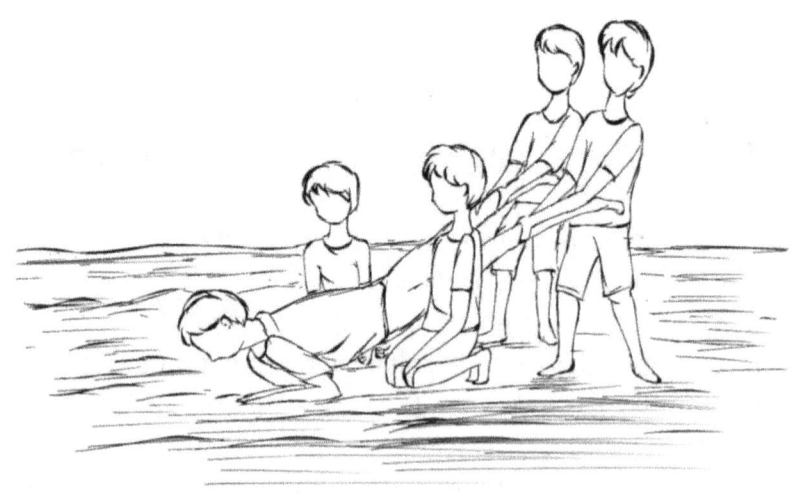

51. Kaaker Deem Khela (Crow's Eggs Game)

This is a game where children pretend to be crows. No set number of players is required for this game; however, the minimum is at least three.

First, one player is selected to be the *moochi* (cobbler) by playing "rock-paper-scissors." The rest of the players are the crows. After the selection of the cobbler, players draw a line on the ground and stand behind that line. Then the cobbler chooses a random player by saying to them, *"Tor paayer tole kaaker deem"* (There are crow's eggs under your feet). Hearing that, the selected player must stand on one foot, keeping the other off the ground so as to not crush the "eggs." The player must continue to keep one leg folded up behind them, but they may support it by holding it with one hand.

While the selected player is standing on one leg, the cobbler recites the following rhyme:

> *Paayer tole kaaker deem.* (Crow's eggs under the feet.)
>
> *Bhaanglo keda? Jahangir.* (Who smashed it? It's Jahangir.)

If the targeted player fails to keep their leg up or accidentally lets it down, the cobbler tries to tag them immediately. If the cobbler can tag them while they have both legs on the ground, that player becomes the cobbler in the next round. The previous cobbler joins the others and becomes another crow.

The cobbler can target multiple players at the same time or each of the players one by one. The child must continue playing the role of cobbler and keep saying the rhyme until they are able to tag someone else to take the role. It is hard for young children to stay on one leg for long, so the cobbler stays vigilant to see who fails. The cobbler may also make sudden movements or say part of the rhyme loudly to startle the players into making mistakes.

52. Boora-Boorir Khela (The Old Man and Woman Game)

This is another game of acting. Two boys usually do the acting, but it is not a fixed rule. The two players act as an elderly peasant couple. The old lady is upset with her husband, and the husband is teasing her playfully. Young children usually put on quite a show, with extravagant costumes and funny gestures to make it more comical for the audience. The child who plays the husband may use limestone mixed with water to make their hair white. They also wear a fake mustache made of dried, concentrated chert on jute fibers. The child who plays the old lady wears a *shari* (a traditional Indian dress for women) and a veil over their head.

This game is popular in Bangladeshi villages as the villagers there are more familiar with this type of couple and their lover's quarrels. The story of a couple who have grown old together but whose affection hasn't faded for each other over time has an exceptional hold on the audience. The sweet, loving gestures mixed with funny and dramatic execution keep the audience's attention throughout.

The performance starts with a scene where the old lady slowly walks into her yard while leaning on a stick and chewing a betel leaf. The child who plays that role shakes their hands and moves slowly to seem like a very old person. Then, the husband enters, ready to go farming with a yoke on his shoulder like a farmer. Children will use some other object and pretend it's a yoke, as a real yoke is quite heavy. Then, the husband strikes up a conversation with his wife that goes something like this:

Husband: *Bhaat raindha deeba toomi, haal baite jaabo aami.* (I'm going to plow. Cook rice for me.)

Wife: *Bhaat raante paarmu na, baaper baari jaimu gaa.* (I won't cook rice. I will leave you and go back to my father's home.)

Husband: *Baaper baari jaiba toomi chool dhoira aanmu aami.* (If you go to your father's home, I'll bring you back pulling you by your hair.)

Wife: *Chool dhoira aanba toomi, dhom dhoira thaakmu aami.* (If you pull me by my hair, I'll be upset with you and give you the silent treatment.)

Husband: *Dhom dhoira thaakona toomi, kaan dhoira taanbo aami.* (If you do that with me, I'll pull your ear.)

Wife: *Kaan dhoira taanona toomi. Khoo khoo deeya polaimu aami!* (Just come and try to pull my ear. I'll run away instantly!)

Husband: *Khoo khoo deeya polaiba toomi, chool dhoira taanbo aami.* (You won't escape me. I'll catch you by your hair.)

Wife: *Chool dhoira taanle toomi, aagoone pooiraa mormu aami.* (If you pull my hair, I'll jump on fire and kill myself.)

Husband: *Aagoone pooiraa morba toomi tomaar shathe mormu aami.* (If you die, I'll die with you.)

The elderly couples of the village like to make playful threats to tease each other. It is their way of expressing love. The game ends with the couple making peace. The audience claps for the entertaining performance and the happy ending.

53. Dhaan Nere Deya Khela (Rice Drying Game)

Dhaan Nere Deya Khela is a game about processing rice paddy. In this game, young children mimic the process of letting paddy dry in the yard. Children act as adult women who work in the yard to prepare the paddy by drying it in the sun before threshing. Children like to mimic adults, and young girls like to observe their mothers and other village women working alongside their farmer husbands to prepare paddy to make rice. They also know how important this work is, which inspires them to become adults and do significant things themselves. These interests are expressed through this acting game.

At the beginning of the game, eight to ten teenage girls wave their hands and imitate letting the paddy dry in the yard. They wear *shari* like grown women wear while working in an attempt to imitate the adult women's activities completely. They wrap the hem of the *shari* tightly around their waist, and sometimes they pull a veil over their head. Or sometimes they just stare up at the sky without the veil and sigh as if tired after working for hours.

While playing the game, young girls sometimes add something extra to reflect the customs of their village. In peasant families, the sons' wives work together in the yard. In some families, the strict and old mother-in-law inspects the wives' work to ensure they are not slacking off. So, the young girls also include these elements in the game. One girl, acting as the mother-in-law, may sit on a low tool and, with great focus, cut betel nuts, smash them using a mortar and pestle, and then pretend to put them in her toothless mouth while continuously moving her jaw.

While acting, the players make conversation that goes something like this.

Mother-in-law: *Kee koren roi?* (What are you doing?)

Wives: *Dhaan naari dei.* (I am laying the paddy.)

Mother-in-law: *Guiaa khaya jao.* (Come here and have some betel nuts.)

Wives: *Chaagol baandi aage.* (Let me tie up the goats first.)

Then, some girls make sounds like rumbling thunder with their mouths. Hearing the sound of thunder, the mother-in-law realizes that it might start raining, so she starts screaming to warn her daughters-in-law:

Jhori aailo roi! Jhori aailo! Dhaan tolo roi Dhaan tolo! (The storm is coming! The storm is coming! Go quickly, bring the paddy into the house!)

Then, the girls who were making the thunder sounds start to set the scene of rain. To do this, they take water in their mouth and spit it up toward the sky. Hearing the mother-in-law's shouting, one of the wives comes running and pretends to pick up the paddy quickly, and the game ends here. This game is popular in the Pabna and Rangpur districts.

Agriculture is an essential part of the economy of Bangladesh, and paddy is a staple food in this region. Cultivating rice and everything related to it plays a vital role in the everyday life of common villagers. Producing rice is not easy, and only those who do farm labor realize how difficult it is to store rice at home after harvesting it from the field. Aush paddy ripens in the rainy season when it must be cut, threshed, dried, and sown later. The rural women's unparalleled hard work and dedication to doing this work is indescribable. In the unbearable heat, their whole body sweats. The rains come suddenly and repeatedly—sometimes in torrents, sometimes in drizzle. So, these women have to stay very alert to the skies. They constantly have to lay rice to dry in the sun, then quickly take it into the house when it rains, and then repeat this process. Children, especially girls, who grow up observing this tireless hard work, learn to value and respect these women and their diligence.

54. Dhekibhana Khela (Husking Paddy Game)

Dhekibhana Khela is another game related to cultivating rice. This one represents the latter process of threshing paddy after drying it out. Girls play this game by pretending to husk paddy with a *dheki* (see image) like the adult women of the village while reciting this poem:

Dheki koor koor. (The *dheki* goes "*kur kur.*")
Beeraya aashook dhaan re. (Let the rice come out.)
Dheki koor koor. (The *dheki* goes "*kur kur.*")
Naai tor choukh kaan re. (You don't have a nose or eyes.)
Dheki koor koor. (The *dheki* goes "*kur kur.*")
Hobe taarataari re. (Let the rice be done quickly.)
Dheki koor koor. (The *dheki* goes "*kur kur.*")
Hoiya geche dhaan re! (There! The rice is done!)
Aleyar maay dhaan bhaane. (Aleya's mom is threshing rice.)
Aleyay khay khood. (Aleya eats *khood*. Note: *Khood* is the residue from threshing rice or the broken rice.)
Gaab gaache morog daake koot koot kooroot. (Up in the persimmon tree, the rooster goes "*koot koot kooroot.*")

55. Pootul Khela (Playing Dolls)

Playing with dolls is a common children's game in many parts of the world. In Bangladesh, it is played in many different ways, and the dolls also come in different varieties. The most common ones are made with rags that the children make themselves. The rags can be of different colors but are mostly white.

Children make bride and groom dolls and marry the couples by arranging a complete wedding ceremony with food, guests, and festive decorations. In the villages of Bangladesh, a traditional marriage ceremony is usually celebrated with great splendor, and it is a delightful occasion for children as they get to enjoy music, dance, delicious foods, and so on. So, re-creating the celebration with dolls is an exciting activity for them. They make the food and decorations using their creativity and imagination, which adds extra fun. They usually make the festival dishes from sand and mud—the most readily available materials—but the materials used can vary. For the plates to serve the meals, they use banana leaves, jackfruit leaves, banyan leaves, etc. Sometimes the guests for the ceremony are other children, and sometimes the guests are their dolls. The children sit in rows, pretending to eat the food, and wash their hands and face after eating. When they use their dolls as guests, they pretend as if the dolls are eating the food with great delight.

They also use rhymes in this game, which are usually about the marriage ceremony. The rhyme begins with the groom coming to take the bride, but she is shy and anxious to leave her parents' home. Her parents and relatives are crying. Even her cat is sad! The rhyme ends with everyone blessing the couple with a happy marital life. The story of the marriage ceremony and accompanying drama represent a traditional picture of Bangladeshi village life, cultural values, and societal norms.

Other than marrying the dolls, which is the most common way of playing, children also love to play with dolls by making up conversations between them, acting out different scenarios they see in everyday life. Children also use dolls just to cuddle them to sleep. Even babies are happy to have their own dolls. Dolls become children's constant companions and friends.

Puppets or dolls are also a major part of Bangladeshi folk culture. Many different materials have been used to make dolls, such as clay, jute, yarn, wood, stone, Indian cork, cane, bamboo, bronze, silver, copper, buffalo horn, ivory, and paper pulp. Potters use their fingers to make the dolls by pressing clay and giving them a flat head, lips like birds, and other shapes like hands and legs. They create ornaments on the dolls with painted clay twine.

Over the years, there have been significant changes in doll-playing traditions, including the materials used to create them, the structure, shape, and nature of the dolls, and the stories they are used to portray. These days, several different types of dolls are being produced and sold. They design dolls in a combination of local and foreign modern styles as well as age-long traditional styles.

Part II:
Outdoor Games

There are many outdoor games in Bangladesh. Some have been influenced by other cultures, and some originated in the Bengali culture. Most outdoor games are played on a daily basis by children who are looking to get outside, meet up with friends, and have lots of fun.

Chapter 1: Simple Outdoor Games Without Props or Toys

56. Phooltokka Khela (Flicking on the Forehead Game)

Phooltokka Khela is very popular among young girls. An equal number of players on two teams compete in this game. Each team has a leader called *raaja* (king), and before the competition starts, the kings must select the players for their teams. Both kings want to get smart, intelligent, and athletic players for their teams. However, a random selection method is used so that neither of the kings can take all the best players for their team.

To choose the players for each team, the players (other than the kings) must go some distance away and make pairs among themselves. Then, the pairs each choose a pseudonym of two names (e.g., flower-fruit, mango-jam, sky-wind) for themselves and return to the kings.

> Then, each pair stands before the kings and says, "*Daak daak isko.*" (Call, call us this.)
> Both kings reply: *Aami Mari Misko.* (I am Marie Misko.)
> The pair responds: *Ke nebe aakaash, ke nebe baataash?* (Who will take the sky? Who will take the wind?)

With this last line, the pair mainly asks the kings to choose one pseudonym for their team. The pseudonym can be anything other than wind and sky. This way, the kings will have a random player for their team. However, sometimes naughty children try to cheat to get into their favorite king's team by making suggestive gestures to that king. To avoid this, all players keep a close watch, and if someone gets caught cheating, it leads to quarreling. Nonetheless, there are some that always try cheating, adding extra excitement to the game.

After the teams are formed, two long lines are marked on the ground, leaving a space of about eight to nine feet between them. The bigger the space in the middle, the more interesting the game can become. The kings stand face-to-face with their teammates on either side of the two lines. Then, the game begins.

The kings discuss the game strategy with their teammates and decide on pseudonyms for all their players. Then, the king from Team A goes over to Team B's line and randomly chooses one player. King A stands behind the chosen player and places their hands over that player's eyes, covering their vision. Then, King A calls over one of their own players using their given pseudonym.

King A says, "*Ay re aamar golaap ay re.*" (Come here my rose, come here.)

The player who was given the name *golaap* (rose) comes forth, lightly flicks the opponent player's forehead, and quietly goes back behind their team's line. King A then uncovers the opponent player's eyes, and that player has to guess who flicked their forehead. The members of Team A all keep their expressions neutral so the opposing player can't tell who the culprit is. Sometimes, they even try to misguide the person. For example, the one who didn't flick pretends like they are guilty or avoids eye contact. Naive players sometimes fall for the bluffing and choose the wrong person. If that happens, the one who actually flicked the forehead wins.

The winning player then gets to squat on their team's marked line and make one big leap forward, like a frog. They can occupy the area as far as they can jump. However, if the player who was flicked can identify the correct flicker, then this player gets to leap instead. The turn then goes to Team B, and their king plays similarly. At the end of the turn, another player gets to leap. This way, each team tries to occupy as much space in the middle as possible and compete against each other. The team that occupies the most area wins the game. After each turn, the kings can change the names of their teammates if they like. However, the same name can't be chosen twice.

There are different names for this game in the different regions of Bangladesh. The game is known as *Tokaatooki* (Flicking) in the Mymensingh region, *Golaap-Togor* (Rose-Crape Jasmine Flowers) in the Kushtia region, and *Orna Khela* (Scarf Game) in the Rajshahi region.

57. Bou-chi (Don't Let Her Escape!)

Bou-chi or *Boori-chi* is a common game that is mainly played by girls in both rural villages and larger towns. There are hardly any Bangladeshi women who haven't played this game at some point in their childhood. In the villages, it used to be common to see young girls happily playing this game in the yards in the soft late afternoon light. Unfortunately, as times change and children's outdoor playing spaces are decreasing, this game is on the brink of extinction.

Bou-chi involves a lot of running, jumping, and sprinting. So, this game also provides healthy exercise for young girls. Depending on the part of the country where this game is played, it goes by many different names. For example, the game is known as *Chi-Raani* in the Chittagong region, *Khoom* in the Noakhali region, *Chi-Boori* in the Barisal region, and *Boorir Chi* in the Khulna region. Some of the other names that this game goes by are *Boorikaapaati*, *Bou-baashonti*, and *Boorir choo*. Despite its many names, the style of play is almost the same everywhere. However, since rhymes are used in this game, there can be regional variations in the rhymes as well.

This game is played between two teams. The leaders of the teams are called *raaja*, or king, like in the game *Phooltokka Khela*. Every team has an equal number of players, usually ten to twelve children. The way that the leaders choose players for their team is also the same as in *Phooltokka Khela*.

After the team members are selected, the players must decide which team will get the first turn. A leaf is used to resolve this matter. Each team chooses one side of the leaf, and whichever team's side of the leaf falls on the ground, that team wins the first chance to play.

This game requires two courts to be drawn on the ground, one rectangular and the other circular, twenty-five to thirty feet apart from each other. One player from the team that will go first is chosen to play the *bou* (bride) and goes inside the circle court (in some games, instead of a bride, it is a *boori* (old lady)). The remaining members of the bride's team go inside the rectangular court.

The goal of the *bou* is to escape her circle (her cell) and join the players of her team in the rectangular court. The opposing team tries to stop her from doing so. Her team members, one by one, must hold their breath and chant rhymes while trying to tag the players on the opposing team. If a player manages to tag anyone from the opposing team, that player gets disqualified from the game. Thus, the *bou*'s team tries to decrease the number of players from the opposing team so that the bride can escape. However, if they run out of breath and any opponent tags them, the person who ran out of breath will be disqualified instead. Whenever a player from the bride's team starts the chase, the opposing player starts darting around so that it is more challenging for their pursuer to hold their breath. However, there is a limited space in which they can run, so they can only go so far. While running around, the opposing team also has to make sure that the bride doesn't escape her cell.

While trying to escape her cell, if the bride gets tagged by the opposing team, then the bride's team loses. If all of their team members get tagged, their team will lose too. So, the goal of the bride's team is to rescue the bride without losing all their team members, and the goal of the opposing team is to keep the bride inside the circle without losing all their members.

The opposing team will win if they manage to keep the *bou* inside the circle for a specific time duration. The players decide on the duration prior to the start of the game.

58. Open to Bioscope (Garland Wearing Game)

Open to Bioscope is one of the most popular Bengali traditional games. There is not a single person who does not have a childhood memory of this game. Young children playing this game together in the lazy afternoon is a very common and beautiful scene in Bangladesh.

To start, two players are randomly selected using an *ootha* (hat) to be the kings. They stand facing each other, raise their arms in the air, and join them together to form an arch, locking their fingers together (see image). The other players then form a line and walk under this arch (or gate), holding onto the person in front of them by the shoulders or waist. The two kings (gatekeepers) say a rhyme together while the other players cross through the gate.

The rhyme goes like this:

Open to Bioscope.

Nine ten Telescope.

Chooltaana beebiana.

Shaaheb Baaboor boithok khaana. (Living room of a gentleman and his wife.)

Shaaheb boleche jete paan shoopaari khete. (The gentleman has invited me there to eat betel nut.)

Paaner aagae morich baata. (There is pepper paste on the end of the betel.)

Spring er chaabi aata. (There are keys tucked in the key chain.)

Jaar naam Renoobaala taake debo mooktaar maala. (I will give a pearl necklace to the one who is named Renubala.)

As soon as the pearl necklace part is said, the player who is at the gate (under the hands of the two kings) is captured. The kings bring their arms down on the player as if they are putting a garland on that player. The player will then need to leave the line and stand aside. The two kings will start saying the rhyme again, and the players will continue to walk under their outstretched arms. Another player will be caught upon reciting the pearl necklace part.

Sometimes, this game is played as a part of another game like *Phooltokka Khela*. Every time a player is given the garland, the kings take them aside and ask them to choose one pseudonym. What they say will dictate which king's team they will belong to. The specific rhyme used in this game has different variations in the different regions.

Hide-and-Seek Games

59. Polaapoli Khela

Polaapoli Khela is the traditional "Hide and Seek" game, similar to other games of this nature around the world. *Polaapoli* is a local variation on the Bengali word *lookaano* (hiding). This term is used in the Rangpur, Barisal, Pirojpur, Bhola, and Jessore districts. There are also other names for this game with slight differences in the gameplay. In the Noakhali district, it is called *Chokhpolaani Khela,* and in Chattogram, the name is *Koolook Khela* (see below). This game is a favorite of children in both villages and towns. In towns, though, there is another version of this game called "*Teelo-Express*" (see below).

One player is chosen through a toss to become the *chor* (thief). The *chor* then closes their eyes and starts counting, giving time to the other players to hide somewhere. In towns, children hide behind curtains, under beds, behind *aalmeeraahs* (cupboards or wardrobes), or in other places in their houses or apartments. In villages, the options for hiding are even more plentiful. Children hide in trees, on the roofs of houses, behind bushes, inside piles of hay, and so on.

After counting to a set number, the thief looks for the hiding players. If the thief can catch the players in a certain amount of time, those players lose. The first one to be caught plays the thief in the next round. The ones who don't get caught in that time frame win. Children take great joy in hiding creatively and not getting caught.

60. Polaantook/Chor-Chor Khela

In the *Polaantook* game, the gameplay is the same as in the *Polaapoli* game. However, in this game, the *chor* (thief) is chosen through a fun rhyming game. To do this, children make a circle, standing side by side. Then, each player recites one line of a poem written for this game and touches the person standing next to them. Whoever is touched on the last line leaves the circle. This process repeats until there is only one player left in the circle, and that player becomes the thief.

The rhyme goes like this:

Elating Belating Telating Chor
Myfore before thirty-four
Ishteeshoner mishti kool (Sweet palm fruits in the train station)
Shokher baagan golaap phool (Flower from my fancy garden)
Kaaker golaay *kontho maala* (The crow is wearing garlands)
Bang baajaay beena (The frog is playing a harp)
Shotti kore jabo mago (Oh mother, I promise)
Mokka Modeena (I'll go to Makka and Madina)

The first two lines of the rhyme are just nonsense words to rhyme the rest of the lines, and the rhyme itself isn't really related to the game. It is just a random verse that children came up with. However, this rhyme expresses the simple things in village life that children love as well as the desire of many Muslim children to visit the sacred religious places of great value to them. The *Polaantook* game is also called the *Elating Belating* game from the first words of the rhyme and *Chor-Chor Khela* in some regions.

There is also another way to choose who plays *chor*. Jackfruit leaves are placed in a pile according to the number of players, and one slightly torn leaf is hidden in the pile. All players randomly pick a leaf, and whoever picks the torn one becomes the thief. Children then say a rhyme to tease the thief. The rhyme usually contains lines like "The thief is wearing a silly costume." Then, everyone randomly ends the lyrics with a wish that they want to eat jackfruit. Repeating that line, they start singing and dancing, and, while doing that, they begin to scatter around and hide. After hiding, they have to make a sound like "*took*" or "*too*," and then the thief knows where to start looking for them. Sometimes, the players tease the thief by not making any sound at all. The players find this amusing as the thief gets flustered. After the thief finds all the hidden players, the game restarts by choosing another *chor* in the same way.

The ending verse of the rhyme for this game mentions that all players want to eat jackfruit. Jackfruit is the national fruit of Bangladesh and a favorite fruit of most people in the country. The props for this version of the game are also jackfruit leaves, which reflect the ending of the rhyme.

61. Koolook Khela

This version of *Polaapoli Khela* is played mainly in the Chattogram district. Children form two teams—one that will hide and one that will seek. The members of the hiding team will hide themselves in different places inside a house while the other team waits outside. After the hiding is done, the members of the hiding team give a signal by shouting *"koolook,"* which is different from the signal in *Polaantook*. As such, the game is named after this signal. The ones who get found must go outside the house, and the roles are reversed. Thus, the game continues with a great deal of liveliness.

62. Teelo-Express

In towns, *Teelo-Express* is played a bit differently. In this game, one player has to hide, and all the others need to find them. After being chosen randomly by a toss, the selected player goes to hide. Once in their hiding place, that player shouts "Ready," and the other players go to look for them. The first person who finds them must say "Express," and then they win and get to be the next player to hide. However. if, before saying "Express," the player in hiding can say *"Teelo,"* then that player wins and gets the opportunity to hide again. Thus, the game continues.

63. Eeri-Beeri Khela

Eeri-Beeri Khela is another hide-and-seek game played a little differently than the previous ones. In the *Eeri-Beeri* game, the one who is 'It' or *chor* (thief) is chosen in an interesting way. First, the number of players participating in the game is counted. Then one person uses a tree branch or stone to write each of these numbers on the soft ground, out of the sight of the other players. Then, the person who wrote the numbers covers the numbers with objects like broken pieces of wood, stones, leaves, etc. When this is done, the other players return, and each chooses one hidden number randomly. The one who wrote the numbers on the ground gets the last number remaining.

Whoever chooses the number one becomes the thief. This person starts reciting a special rhyme made just for this game, while everyone else goes to hide.

The verse goes like this:

Eeri-Beeri Binnath

Teeri beeri gaach (Crooked trees)

Baarir pechone Tetool gaach (There is a tamarind tree)

Jaare shekhane paamu (Whoever I find there)

Ghaar bhangiya khaamu (I'll grab you by the neck and gobble you up)

Chaarlaam daak! (Here I go! I'm going to start calling for you!)

Lookaiya thaak! (You better stay hidden wherever you are!)

The rhyme begins with random names of paddy plants—*Eeri-Beeri* and *Binnath*. Like other local games, this game is named after the first words of the rhyme. The rhyme usually contains amusing content with playful threats to the players hiding. It says that they better stay hidden because if the *chor* finds them, they will be done for. In some regions, the thief also pretends to "gobble up" the players after catching them, which becomes amusing for little children.

To win, the thief has to touch the player after finding them, and then that person becomes the thief in the next round. However, if the thief can't find a hiding player, another player can come out from their hiding place and, while the thief is not looking, sneakily touch that hiding player. If this happens, then the thief loses and must maintain their role in the next round. The game continues until all players are caught. This game can be played in both small and large outdoor areas.

Games of Tag

Most people around the world should be familiar with the concept of the game of tag. In Bangladesh, there are many games similar to the basic game of tag, each with slight variations.

64. Kaabadi or Haa-doo-doo Khela

Kaabadi, informally known as *Haa-doo-doo Khela,* is the national game of Bangladesh and is highly popular among children and adults alike. The fighting spirit and huge popularity of this game are the contributing factors to the game's popularity.

The Bengali word *haa-doo-doo* may have originated from the Bengali word *haatoo* (knee). This game has different regional names such as *Hoothoot, Voodu, Kaabadi, Gootoogootoo, Doogdoog, Chhedoogoor, Chikhela, Doogoodoonood, Oomaali, Haamaali, Kaapaati,* and *Tektek.* It is known as *Chinchaaraani* in the Mymensingh district, *Chaand* in Rajshahi, and *Paatti* in Rangpur and Dhaka. This game is usually played on occasions such as *Mohorrom* (The Muslim New Year), *Eid-ul-Fitr* and *Eid-ul-Azha* (two major Islamic ceremonies), *Pohela Boishakh* (Bengali New Year), and Independence Day. It is mainly played in the rainy season when the soil on the ground is soft from the rainwater. This way, the intense fighting can be played out properly and without many injuries.

Haa-doo-doo consists of two teams with seven or eight players; however, the number of players is flexible. The game may be played in one of two ways: 1) *Kotabondi* (bound in court), the game is played by marking boundaries on the ground and 2) *Chhaara Kaapaati* (saying rhymes), the game is played without boundaries.

The game of *Kotabondi* (bound in court) focuses on the court dimensions. The length and width of this court is 21 x 14 feet, respectively. The court is divided into two equal parts by a straight line in the middle. This middle line has different names such as *"gaang"* in Khulna, *"khaan"* in Jessore, *"ded"* in Kushtia, and others. On both sides of the court, an equal number of players from both teams take attacking and defensive positions. During the *Kotabondi* game, maintaining the game inside the boundary is necessary.

To begin, one player takes in a deep breath of air and, while holding it, darts forward onto the side of their opponent, attempting to tag as many players as possible before running out of breath. The player must continuously repeat the word *"haa-doo-doo"* or *"kaabadi"* to prove they still have breath left. If the runner manages to tag players and return to their side without losing all their breath, the tagged players will be dismissed from the game. But if the runner runs out of breath before returning to their court, they will be the one dismissed. Also, if the runner crosses back over the middle line while trying to tag opponents, the opposing team can trap them in a lock. The runner will have to get out of the lock while holding their breath to avoid getting dismissed from the game. The team that dismisses the most opposing players wins. Some rhymes, which can vary depending on the region, are also said during the game.

Winning this highly competitive game is a matter of honor for villagers and has even led to the evolution of some superstitions. Many believe in magic and try to use it to win the game. The villagers hire a *Kobiraaj* (a learned individual with magical and medicinal knowledge) to save their teams from falling victim to magical tricks. The *Kobiraaj* recites the following mantra and gives them *tel pora* (magical oil that is believed to have certain powers):

Tel toolshi paak tel fotiker aashay. (Tulsi oil, holy oil for the hope of winning.)

Haate khooshi mookhe khooshi indropoorer raajar. (I apply it on the hand, on the face of the King of Indripur.)

Moddhe boshi jei tel pora deelaam. (I blew magic on the oil and gave the magic oil to you.)

It is believed that if the magical oil is applied to the face and body in a counterclockwise direction, any magic applied by the opponent will be neutralized during the game. Additionally, if someone urinates on the field without anyone noticing, any negative effect of the opponent's *tontro-montro* can also be removed.

65. Borof-Paani Khela (Ice-Water Game)

Borof-Paani Khela (similar to "Freeze Tag") is a game of tag where one player or "thief" is chosen at the beginning of the game and chases everyone, trying to tag them. In tagging a player, the thief turns players into "ice." That is, if the thief touches someone, they have to stop and act like they are frozen on the spot. If an unfrozen player comes and touches a frozen player, the frozen player will turn back into water and be free to run again. If the thief manages to freeze everyone (at the same time), the one who was turned to ice first will become the new thief.

Another similar game is called *Choachui Khela* (Game of Tag). However, in this case, the thief doesn't try to freeze the players. Rather, the thief has to tag a player while holding their breath and then return to a particular place or house ("home base"). If the thief is successful, then the player who got tagged will be the next thief. If the thief runs out of breath and someone catches them and tags them before reaching home base, the same player will continue to be the thief for the next round.

66. Aalooni Chaaloon Khela

There isn't a fixed number of players for the *Aalooni Chaaloon* game, but the more players there are, the merrier the game becomes. Similar to the Game of Tag *(Choachui Khela)*, in this game, one player is "It," and they are called *chor* (thief) or sometimes *moochi* (cobbler).

The game starts with choosing who will be the thief. The thief is selected using a method similar to "rock-paper-scissors" called *haat shaakkhi deya* (giving testimony through hands).

The game is generally played in a yard or under a tree. The players draw two circles about five to six feet apart on the ground. Everybody stands inside one circle except the thief, who stands outside and says, "*Aalooni Chaaloon, Khoi Chaaloon*" (Tasteless food or toasted paddy). Note: *Khoi* is a tasty Bengali food that is prepared by frying rice grain.

Upon hearing the thief, the children start running in various directions, trying to reach the circle at the other end without getting tagged by the thief. If anyone gets tagged, they become the thief in the next round, and the previous thief joins the other players.

The name of this game comes from the first words uttered by the thief. This game is popular in the Magura district in Bangladesh.

67. Tekra Tekri

Two teams with equal players and a leader are required for this game. The leader of each team is called *raaja* (king). Two circles are drawn on opposite ends of the playing area. One circle is the starting point, and the other is the finishing point (goal). One team (Team A) is chosen through a toss and stands in the starting circle. The first round starts on a mark, and Team A starts running in different directions, trying to reach the finishing point without getting tagged by opposing players. Whoever gets tagged gets dismissed from that round. If anyone can reach the finishing area without being tagged, the team gets one point, and that player can't score any more points in that round. If the leader (king) successfully reaches the goal, the team gets five points. Also, Team B members can't knock out or dismiss Team A players while they are still inside the starting circle, but all players must leave the circle for the first round to be completed. However, if anyone from Team A touches a player of Team B while standing in the circle, that player will be out. The round ends when either the leader is tagged or the leader reaches the goal.

After playing this game for a preset number of rounds, the team with the most points wins.

There is another game with a similar gameplay called *Ontaa Khela*. The only difference is that there isn't any finishing circle, as the goal is to dismiss as many opposing players as possible to win. The chasing team runs while holding their breath, trying to tag opposing players. However, if someone on the chasing team loses their breath and gets tagged out instead, they get teased by their teammates.

68. Maangsho Choori Khela (Meat Stealing Game)

This game is about stealing and protecting an imaginary piece of meat. In the game, there are two teams of four or six players—one team that tries to steal the meat (the thieves) and the other team that defends it (the guards). Children use a piece of brick as the "meat." A line is drawn on the ground, and the two teams stand on either side.

The guards begin with the meat on their side of the line (their court), usually 30-40 feet from the opponent's position. The thieves have to cross the line, get to the meat, take it back to their court, and tag as many players from the guard team as possible to dismiss them from the game—all in one breath. Thieves sometimes say rhymes or random, meaningless words like "*cchi*" or "*choo*" to show they haven't lost their breath. Covering the long distance and doing everything in one breath is challenging. Therefore, the guards keep a keen eye on their opponents' breathing. If a thief takes a breath, the guards chase them, trying to tag them. If tagged, that player will be dismissed from the game. If the tagged player has taken the meat, it will be returned to the guards. However, if a thief brings the meat home successfully, the thieves' team will get one point.

The game continues for a specific time or until all players from either team are dismissed. In the next round, the roles are reversed, and the game is played again. The team with the most points wins the game.

69. Aaloo-Aaloo Khela (Potato-Potato Game)

Aaloo-Aaloo Khela is another version of *Maangsho Choori Khela.* However, in this game, players use a potato (*aaloo*) instead of a make-believe piece of meat. Also, in addition to tagging players out, the guard team can try to drag a thief inside their court and dismiss them when they run out of breath. Another difference is that instead of saying "*cchi*" or "*choo*," the thief has to continuously say a rhyme to prove they still have breath.

The rhyme goes like this:

> *Aaloo aaloo khelte gele maa kore maana.* (Mother forbids me from playing the potato-potato game.)
>
> *Haat paa bhenge gele jaabo daaktrkhaana.* (Because I will have to go to the hospital if I break my arms and legs.)

70. Sandel Choori Khela (Sandal Thief Game)

Sandel Choori Khela is also very similar to *Mangsho Choori Khela*. However, in this case, the players use their sandals instead of the make-believe meat. Two teams play this game; one is thieves, and the other is the guards.

In this game, as in some others mentioned, the teams have leaders who choose their teammates randomly. The players approach them in pairs and ask the leaders to choose one of the pseudonyms the players have created for themselves. The leaders do not know which pseudonym corresponds to which player. This way, the leaders can't choose the players they want for their team.

The team to play the thieves is decided by a toss. Then the thieves start to run, one by one while holding their breath, to steal the sandals and tag out the guards.

The first player from the thief team to start the game says the following rhyme:

Prothom tip deete gelaam. (I'm leaving for the first go.)

Shobaike jaaniye gelam. (I'm letting everyone know.)

The other thieves recite similar rhymes when it is their turn to snatch sandals.

If a thief runs out of breath, the guards can tag them out as well. Tagged players from either team are dismissed from that round only. A round is completed after all the sandals have been brought over to the thieves' court or all players from either team have been dismissed. In the next round, the team roles are reversed. For each sandal successfully stolen, the thief team gets one point. After playing for a determined number of rounds, the team scoring the most points wins.

71. Haabba-Daabba Khela

In this game, first, a thief is chosen through an elaborate five-step process. To do this, all players sit in a circle. In the first step, they all say "*haabba*" together and place the palm of their right hand on top of the palm of their left hand. In the second step, they flip both hands, keeping them together, and say "*daabba*." In the third step, they move the thumb of one hand onto the palm of the other and say "*kolshi*" (a type of water pitcher). For the fourth step, they place one elbow on the palm of the other hand and say "*koni*" (elbow). For the last step, they place the palms of both hands on their head and say "*maatha*" (head). Everyone must follow the process and utter the correct words for each step together. The first player to make a mistake, either by failing to keep up with everyone or by not saying the right words at the same time as the others, becomes the thief. If more than one player makes a mistake at the same time, those players go through the five-step process again to determine the thief.

The thief then stands inside a circle drawn on the ground while the others remain outside it. The thief has to leave the circle and try to tag the players outside the circle. Whoever is tagged first becomes the thief in the next round. However, if at least half of the opposing players can get inside the circle while the thief is outside it, the thief continues being the thief in the next round. So, the thief's challenge is to stay close to the circle while still trying to tag players out. But all the players running in different directions make it hard for the thief to do this.

72. Gollaachhoot (Circle Run)

Gollaachhoot is a popular game and is still familiar throughout Bangladesh today. However, unfortunately, it has started to become lost over time. Children in rural villages play this game on large, empty crop fields where the harvesting has been completed.

A long stick or pole is placed in the center of a small circle on the ground, and this is treated as the starting point of the game. A tree or a stone twenty-five to thirty feet from the center is set as the goal or ending point. The objective is for each player to run from the center circle to the goal. The name of the game comes from the Bangla word for "hole" or "circle" (*gollaa*) and the word for "run" (*chhoot*).

The game is played between two teams of equal numbers of five or seven players. The team leader is called *goda* (chief). To begin, the players mark two sides of the playing field as the starting and ending sides. As mentioned, the starting side is marked with a small circle, usually with a one-foot radius, and the ending point is marked by a tree, a big rock, or a part of a wall about twenty-five to thirty feet away from that circle.

A toss is done to determine which team goes first. Then, that team's leader (chief) goes to stand in the starting circle. The chief moves around the circle with one hand on the long stick in the middle and the other holding another player's hand. That player moves around the circle with the chief while holding yet another player's hand, and thus, all the team's players create a moving chain.

While rotating around the circle, at one point, a player or multiple players at the end of the chain break off from it and start running to reach the goal. The chief may stay inside the circle or run. The objective is to reach the ending side and touch the goal without being tagged. The opposing team positions themselves at random places in the open area of the field. Their objective is to tag the other team's players when they start running and before they reach the goal. Whoever they manage to touch becomes "out" and is dismissed from the game. However, while connected to the chain and circling holding hands, if any player from the chain manages to touch anyone from the opposing team, the player from the opposing team will be out. Like in other games of tag, a player who is tagged "out" cannot participate in the game again until the next round.

Players who successfully reach the goal by running from the starting point are considered "*paaka*" (ripe). A ripe player gets two benefits. First, they are given a chance to jump from the starting circle in the direction of the end line, and a new starting circle will be drawn in the place where that person lands. As a result, their team will be able to start from the new circle, closing the gap between the starting and ending points. Second, ripe players can join the chain again and are eligible to run again. This way, the team can continue to play and advance their starting point closer to the ending point.

When the gap is small enough so that the leader can reach the goal from the starting circle in one jump, the team will win. The leader can also run toward the finish line at any time if they feel they can reach the goal without being touched by any opponents. If the leader is successful, their team will win. However, if the leader gets touched before reaching the goal, then their team will lose. Once the starting team loses, their turn is over, the roles are reversed, and the opposing team gets a turn. As long as a team does not lose, that team can continue playing continual rounds.

73. Kaanamaachi Khela (Blind Bee Game)

Kaanamaachi is similar to the Game of Tag as it also requires one player to become "It" and chase others. However, in this game that player is called the *"Kaana"* (blind one), and that person must chase the others blindfolded. The *Kaana* is chosen through *haat shakkhi deya* (giving testimony through hands), a method similar to "rock-paper-scissors." After the *Kaana* is chosen, they are blindfolded by tying a folded cloth over their eyes. They are asked how many fingers someone is holding up to check if the blindfold was secured properly or not. Then, to confuse the *Kaana* even further, they are spun around a few times.

While spinning the *Kaana*, they sometimes say this rhyme.

Aandha Gondha bhai. (Brother, you are blind.)

Aamar dosh naai. (I have no fault.)

Aami maani aaneena. (I don't know anything.)

Porer chele maaneena. (If it's someone else's son, then I don't care.)

This poem says that if the person is blind but not related to them, this unfortunate situation is not their fault. So, they will tease the blind person and not care about it.

When it is time for the *Kaana* to try to catch the other players, the others surround the *Kaana*, calling out to them and lightly pushing or pinching them from different directions to attract their attention. The *Kaana* tries to catch them by following their sounds and movements. While teasing the *Kaana*, they recite another poem:

Kaanamaachi bho bho. (Blind bee makes buzzing sound, *bho bho.*)

Jaare paabi taare cho. (Touch whom you can.)

The name of the game, *Kaanamaachi Khela* (Blind Bee Game), comes from this poem's first line. The *Kaana* is treated like a blind bee hovering aimlessly to find its prey.

The game continues until the *Kaana* catches a player. After that, the *Kaana* must correctly guess who they caught without seeing them. If they give the wrong answer, they remain as the *Kaana*. However, if they correctly say the name of the player, that player becomes the *Kaana* in the next round. This game is very enjoyable for young children.

This game has ancient origins and is also played in parts of Germany, Persia, India, and southern Canada. This game goes by the name *Aakh Mondon* among the Munda people, an ethnic group in the Indian subcontinent. They play this game as a part of one of their religious rituals, ghost worshipping, which is still prevalent today.

There is another game where one player gets blindfolded called *Kaathi Choachui Khela* (Touching Stick Game). In the Narshingdi district, it is called *Tin Kaathi Khela* (Three Sticks Game). In this game, players stack three sticks horizontally on top of each other in front of a blindfolded player. They then touch one stick, and the blindfolded player has to guess which stick was touched after removing their blindfold.

This is actually not a game of tag, but rather, a game of tricks. The players usually scheme among themselves before tricking other players, often choosing to trick the younger ones. They decide on signs to help the blindfolded player later know which stick was touched. For example, if someone is holding their head in a certain way, it means the top stick was touched. The younger players are amazed when the correct answer is given each time. So, it is also like a game of magic for children. It's fascinating to little kids, but it is no longer fun once the mystery is revealed.

74. Paanir Moddhe Choachui Khela (Water Tag)

Kids can play this game anywhere where they can swim. It can be a pond, river, swimming pool, or other area of water. To begin, one person is chosen to be the *chor* (thief) through a lottery. The thief tries to reach others by swimming and touching them, but everyone else will try to swim away from the thief. Whoever gets touched will become the next thief and try to tag the others.

75. Chikka Khela (Tugging and Tripping Game)

This game of physical endurance is played by two teams of five to seven players. The two teams line up and face each other across a line drawn on the ground. Each player challenges one of the opposing players by stretching their hands toward them in what is known as "giving *haatol*" (handle). The other player catches hold of the outstretched hands, and they start tugging on each other, trying to pull the other over to their side. The one who budges from their position and falls over to the opponent's side is considered "out." This "out" player then becomes a teammate of the opponents and plays for their team in the next round. Both teams try to make the opposing team lose players and increase their own team numbers.

In addition, while tugging, players can also try to free themselves from their opponent's grip and run over to the opponent's side without getting tripped or caught. If a player can successfully run the whole perimeter of the opponent's side without being tripped or caught, they earn one point. This is called earning a *chikka* point, hence the name of the game.

Multiple players can try to pull one opponent to their side at the same time. The players cannot kick, but they can use their feet to loosen the opponent's footing. This is called *lang maara* in Bengali. They can only use their feet to push or pull an opponent's leg to make them lose their balance. A total of three rounds are played. The team that can either dismiss all the opponent's team members or earn more points in two of the three rounds wins.

76. Haaraiya or Loomtoi Khela (Pulling Game)

There is another game similar to *Chikka Khela* which goes by the name *Haaraiya Khela* or *Loomtoi Khela* (Pulling Game).

In this game, the players divide themselves into two teams, Team A and Team B. Team A goes inside a circle drawn on the ground, while Team B stays outside of it. Team A tries to pull Team B into the circle, and Team B tries to resist them. When a player is brought inside the circle, that player has to say the word "*ghorbaana*" (a Bengali word that means "obeying the rules of the house"). If they refuse to say that, they will be kicked or punched. Similarly, Team B must try to pull Team A outside of the circle and make them say "*baarbaana*" (obeying the rules of the outside). The team that can subdue more players from the other team wins.

Young boys mainly play this game as they enjoy proving their physical strength and asserting superiority through this game.

Another game similar to this one goes by the name *Chittaraani Khela*. However, instead of all the team players participating at the same time, the pulling is done by just two players from each team per turn. Also, this game is even more aggressive. Like *Haaraiya Khela*, whichever team manages to defeat the most opposing team players wins the game. *Chittaraani* is also a very hazardous game as there is a risk of severely injuring arms and legs. Sometimes fights break out because of the game as well. The use of wrestling techniques is the main attraction of this version of the game. The players' display of speedy movements and skills makes it worth watching.

77. Noonta Khela (Count to Seven Game)

Noonta means "seven," representing the number of times the rhyme in this game is repeated. The game is played by a single team and is set up by making one player the owner of a large circle that is outlined on the ground.

At the start of the game, everybody goes inside the circle except the owner, who remains outside. The owner walks around the circle reciting the rhyme for this game. When the owner finishes reciting the rhyme, all the players inside the circle cry out, "*Ekre!*" (one).

The owner continues walking around the circle while saying the rhyme again and again, and the players inside the circle keep counting until they reach seven. When the owner finishes reciting the rhyme for the seventh time, all the players inside the circle run out of it, and the owner takes possession of the circle.

However, if the owner steps into the circle while just one player is left inside, the owner will lose the game. The challenge is to step inside right after everybody has left, so the owner has to be quick and good with timing. The other players also have to leave the circle all at once. One or two players can quickly step inside the circle to block the owner from taking possession, but they can't stay in for more than a second.

The players who are trying to block the owner from entering the circle must say, "*noonta*" while stepping back inside the circle, otherwise, the circle will be occupied by the owner. The owner also must say "*noonta*" while taking the circle back.

Noonta Khela is also known as *Kootkoote Khela* in the Jessore and Khulna regions. In that variation, the owner cries out "*Kootaare*" when the others count *ekre* (one), *dooire* (two), *tinre* (three), and so on.

78. Chhi-Chhaattar Khela (The Kite and the Roosters Game)

To play this game, ten to fifteen children form a circle, holding each other's hands, and one player stands in the middle of the circle. In the Rangpur District, the child in the middle is called *chhi* (kite), and the others are *chhaattaar* (roosters). The kite must try to break free from the ring formed by the roosters.

The kite struts around inside the circle and recites a rhyme:

Chhi chhai ghora daabaai! (What a horse I ride!)

Ghora na ghoori? Chaabook chhoodee! (Is it a stallion or a mare? I will whip it!)

Chaabook deeya maarlaam baari dhoola oothe kaarakaari. (When I smack it with a whip, it only raises a row of dust.)

Then, the kite runs out, breaking the circle at a point where someone is not paying attention. The roosters run after the kite, and the one who catches the kite gets to play the kite in the next round.

The roosters also recite a rhyme:

Chhi chhaattaar kaachoor baai? (What is this?)

Chyangra pyangrar naana hoi. (I'm respected as a grandpa by the children.)

Taaker opor ayna. (My bald head shines like a mirror.)

Pooti maachh khai na. (I don't eat Puti fish.) Note: Puti fish is also called Swamp Barb fish.

Taaker opor gosto, Chhuiya dile dosto. (If someone taps on my bald head, I instantly become their friend.)

A variation of this game is played in the Himalayan region where it is known as *Chilla-daoma.*

Chapter 2: Outdoor Games Played with Toys or Props

People in Bangladeshi villages lead a very simple life. During their leisure time, they often come up with various creative games using cheap, available materials that can be found in the natural environment of the villages. Thus, in these places, children can be seen playing games using different local fruits, crops, bamboo, soil, and other readily available products. In many cases, broken or unusable items are utilized or recycled for these games.

79. Tooni Bhai er Tooni Khela (Guess Who Has It!)

This game is well-loved by youngsters in the Chittagong district. When children are at home, they play this game at their leisure to pass the time. This game doesn't have any specific requirements for player numbers, and the gameplay is very easy.

To begin, the children sit in a circle. Everyone puts both of their hands together, keeping a space in the middle of their palms in such a way that something can be hidden inside. Then, two other children stand in the middle of the circle and toss a coin to decide who will get to hide the pebble in someone's hands.

The winner of the coin toss takes turns going around the circle of players, pretending to sneakily put a pebble into each child's hands, while the player who lost the coin toss (their opponent) watches carefully. Everyone sitting in the circle tries to help the person hiding the pebble to deceive their opponent so that they can't tell who really has the pebble. As the player is going around the circle hiding the pebble, that player also says a rhyme.

Once the pebble is hidden, the opponent has to correctly choose who has it. If they can pick the right person, they win. If they fail, the one who hid the pebble wins. The game begins again, and the children in the circle pick two new players to compete against each other in hiding/finding the pebble.

80. Shaat Chaara Khela (Seven Tiles Game)

This game requires an open field, a tennis ball, and at least six players forming two teams, each having three players. Seven *chaara* (pieces of a broken cooking pot) are required for this game, hence the name of the game, *Shaat Chaara* (Seven Tiles). The team to go first is decided by a coin toss.

Before the start of the game, the *chaara* have to be arranged one by one by placing them on top of each other to form a small, tower-like pile (see image). Then, one of the players from the starting team tries to break the pile of *chaara* by throwing a ball from a distance of ten to fifteen feet. The other teammates of the thrower stand near the pile of *chaara*. A player gets a chance to throw the ball seven times in total.

If the ball thrown by the player hits the pile of *chaara* and breaks it, the opposing team can catch the ball and try to hit one of the other team's players with it, like in dodgeball. Meanwhile, the teammates of the player who broke the pile of *chaara*, have to try to avoid getting hit by the ball and, at the same time, set up the pile of *chaara* again. If the opposing team's players successfully hit anyone from the other team with the ball before they finish arranging the pile again, then the throwing team loses their turn, and the opposing team gets a chance to break the pile. If the throwing team manages to set up a new pile without getting hit by the ball, they secure a point, and their turn continues.

81. Naarikel Khela (Coconut Games)

Naarikel or coconut is a very common fruit in South Asia. There are two main types of games in Bangladesh that are played with coconuts.

A. Naarikel Khela 1 (Coconut Game 1)

The first Coconut Game is a competition to remove the coconut skin and break the coconut shell with bare hands without using any tools. Whoever breaks the coconut first wins, and second and third place are also awarded.

If one thinks that a game using fruit may involve wasting food, they are wrong because this game requires players to keep the coconut water drinkable and the pulp edible. As such, they aren't allowed to hit the coconut on the ground or against a tree because, in doing so, the water inside the coconut may spill or it may get contaminated with soil. So, the contestants must first peel the coconut skin off with their teeth or hands and then break the coconut shell with their bare hands. As a result, this game usually tests the strength of the contestants. However, sometimes when the coconut skin is very hard, officials may cut a corner with a knife first, and then let the participants continue with their hands. In general, unripe and softer coconuts that have fallen from the trees are used for this game.

B. Naarikel Khela 2 (Coconut Game 2)

The other version of the Coconut Game is an older, more traditional game which nowadays is almost a lost part of history. However, in a few places in the region, people are still trying to preserve its history by playing this game and teaching it to their children. For example, in the village of Kamata in West Dinajpur (present-day West Bengal Province of India), the Hindus of the Palia community play the Coconut Game every year on *Jonmaashtomy* (the birthday of Sri Krishna, one of the Hindu gods). Also, during *Pooja* (a Hindu religious festival), people gather in the carnival next to the temple to either play the game or watch it from the audience. In front of this huge audience, an intense fight to snatch the coconut begins.

The participants of this game are divided into two teams of ten to twelve. One member of each team (the leader) has a coconut in their hand and holds it tightly to their chest. Players from the opposite team splash water on the person with the coconut and try to snatch it away. This game is similar to American Football or Rugby but with much simpler rules. For example, if the leader of Team A is holding the coconut, then the members of Team B will throw water at that person and try to seize the coconut forcefully from them. At the same time, the other players of Team A will throw water at Team B, trying to protect their leader. If the Team A leader can't hold on to the coconut and the coconut falls to the ground, then the coconut goes to the leader of Team B, and the teams' roles are reversed. However, if a player(s) from Team B can seize the coconut directly from Team A's leader without it falling to the ground, Team B scores one point. The team that scores the most points within a certain timeframe wins and gets to bring the coconut inside the temple as a prize.

82. Hitting with Bamboo Sticks Games

A. Daangooli

Daangooli is quite popular among the rural games of Bangladesh. It used to be a great sensation in the past, but the craze has faded over time.

Wide open spaces are the most suitable for playing *Daangooli*. The game tools consist of a stick made of hard bamboo twigs about two feet long called a *daang* and another about five to six inches long called a *gooli* or *ghooti,* hence the name of the game. The game is also known as *Daangbaadi, Goobaadi, Tyamdaang,* and *Bhyataadaanda,* among others. There is a similar game in Europe called "Tipcat," where the longer stick is used to hit the "cat," or the smaller stick.

A place is marked on the ground as the starting point for the game. Players will stand at the starting point and use the *daang* to hit the *gooli* as far as they can from that point. Two teams with five or six players compete against each other.

The team to hit the *gooli* first is decided through a toss. For example, let's say Team A wins the toss and goes to hit first. Then, Team B will defend. The further a player can hit the *gooli*, the better. When the *gooli* is sent in the air, the opposing team tries to block it by hitting it with another *daang*. If Team B succeeds in blocking the *gooli* or the striking player from Team A fails to hit the *gooli* a minimum distance, that player will be out, and another player from Team A will hit. On the other hand, if Team B fails to block the *gooli*, then Team A will win a point or points, depending on the distance that it traveled, and the hitter will continue to play. All Team A players will get a chance to hit on each turn. After that, it is Team B's turn to strike the *gooli*. The team with the most points in the end wins the game.

There are six rounds in the game, and the technique used to hit the *gooli* is different in each round. The techniques (in order) are: *Muitha, Doori, Teenna, Chairja, Paanja,* and *Kobja.* Each technique is described below:

Muitha: Players must hold the *daang* tightly in one fist and keep one inch out of the fist. The *gooli* should be placed outside of the fist in such a way that it is on the outer side of the *daang.* Then the *gooli* needs to be thrown into the air and hit with the *daang.* There is a high probability of getting out if the player fails to throw the *gooli* up a safe distance.

Doori: In this round, the player holds the *daang* in one hand and the *gooli* in the other with two fingers. The *gooli* has to be thrown lightly in the air and hit with the *daang.*

Teenna: In this round, the player holds the *daang* in one hand and the *gooli* in the other with three fingers. The technique for throwing the *gooli* is the same as in the previous round.

Chairja: The player holds the *daang* like before but now using four fingers to hold the *gooli.* It is necessary to place the *gooli* horizontally by inverting four fingers (the palm of the hand will face up). Then the *gooli* has to be thrown into the air and hit with the *daang.*

Paanja: In this round, the player holds the *daang* the same as before, and the *gooli* has to be placed on the back of the hand while making a fist. Then the player needs to shake their fist lightly to toss the *gooli* into the air and hit it with the *daang.*

Kobja: In this round, the *daang* and *gooli* have to be placed in one hand by holding the *daang* in the fist and placing the *gooli* on the same wrist. The technique of hitting the *gooli* is the same as before.

Method of scoring or counting points in *Daangooli*:

The system of counting points is difficult. If the defending team fails to catch or touch the *gooli* that was hit by their opponent in mid-air, they have to pick up the *gooli* and throw it toward the stick that was driven into the ground at the starting point. If the *gooli* touches the stick, the hitting player is out from that round. If the *gooli* hits the ground only one *daang* length away from the starting point (one *daang* is equal to two feet), the hitting player won't get any score but can remain in the game. But if the player sends the *gooli* further than one *daang* distance, then they will get one point for each extra *daang* distance that the *gooli* travels.

After hitting the *gooli*, a player from the opposing team can try to run toward it and successfully touch it with their *daang*. If they are successful, then the distance between the exact place where they touched the *gooli* with the *daang* and the starting point is measured, and the defending player will get points for each *daang* distance that was covered.

The points earned by a player in each round are recorded. The player wins one "game" when the points reach one hundred in a single round or more.

B. Kodeng

Kodeng is a popular game that is similar to *Daangooli*. The rules of playing *Kodeng* and *Daangooli* are almost the same, however, the starting point of the game is different. In the *Kodeng* game, holes must be dug in the ground, and the *gooli* stick is placed diagonally in a hole. Then, the *gooli* must be hit in a particular way so as to lift it in the air and then beat it forward with a *daang*. The *Kodeng* game is also called *Chaarabaari* or the *Maaittabaari* game.

There are some rules for placing the *gooli* in the hole. The *gooli* must first be placed diagonally in the hole. The part of the *gooli* that protrudes outwards in a semi-vertical position has to be hit with a *daang* tactically so that it goes straight up in the air and is then able to be hit forward.

83. Throwing Skills Games

A. Daigga (Throwing Clay Chunks Game)

This game is all about throwing skills. Players compete against each other to see how far they can make a chunk of clay or hardened soil fly. This game is usually played by two persons, and each player plays with their own piece of clay.

The first one to throw the clay piece is chosen through a toss. This person then throws their piece about fifteen to eighteen feet away from a starting court drawn on the ground. The next player then has two options; they can either try to take away the first piece by hitting it with their own, or they can make their own stance by throwing their piece to another place. If they choose the second option (single throw) they must throw their piece at least fifteen feet.

The game also involves a bit of gambling. Players use bean seeds as game money for betting. The second player to throw usually bets a certain number of beans depending on the option they choose—more beans for hitting the fallen piece and less for making a single throw. If the second player fails to hit the first piece or cover the minimum distance for the single throw, they will lose all the bean seeds they bet to the first player. But if they succeed, they will get the same amount from the other player. Thus, the game continues for a determined number of turns. The player with the most seeds in the end is the winner.

An uneven terrain with high and low places is chosen as the playing field so the clay can fall in the grooves (see image). The idea is that if a player can throw their piece on a higher ground, it becomes trickier for the next player to hit it. Also, while aiming to hit a piece that has fallen on high ground, there is a possibility that the second piece will hit the ground and fall into a lower groove, making it easier for the other player to hit it. Usually, a dried-up pond is the best place for this game as it has multiple low dents in it. So, this game is played primarily in the dry season.

B. Gaaigodaani Khela (Throwing Sticks Game)

Gaaigodaani is a game played by cowherds while tending cows. This game is known as *Phaalaakhaut* in Mymensingh. The sharp, pointy sticks of the cowherds are the main equipment for the game. This game is best played in wet, sticky mud because if the soil is not damp enough, implanting the stick in the soil is difficult. Therefore, selecting such a place for the game is essential. A coin toss is done before the start of the game. The loser is called *gaai* (cow) and is the one to throw the first stick. Implanting sticks in the mud is called *gaam godaani* in Bengali. So, combining the two words *gaai* and *godaani* gives the game its name, *Gaaigodaani*.

The game involves four or five children (usually boys) in a round. The harder and straighter the stick is thrown, the more successfully it can be buried firmly in the ground. If a player cannot do that, they have almost no chance of winning this game. To begin, one player throws their stick so that it sticks into the mud. The next player tries to either knock down the first player's stick or throw their stick so that it is parallel to the first player's stick. If they succeed in doing either of these actions, the second player wins both sticks. But if they fail, the first player wins both sticks. The winner then goes up against the third player to try to win a third stick. This way, the player who can win the sticks of all the players wins the game.

After winning all the sticks, the winner throws the sticks one by one as far away as possible, and the owners run to retrieve theirs. In the meantime, the winner hides their own stick. When the players return with their sticks, they must find the winner's stick and touch it with their own. The one who touches the winner's stick last becomes the new *gaai* (cow) and must go first in the next round.

84. Chel Khela (Finding the Potatoes Game)

This game requires three or more players. To set up the game, one person fills some polythene or discarded packets with sand, soil, or anything similar they can collect. One packet will be filled with several potatoes. The packets must be arranged so no one will be able to tell what is in each packet.

Then, the players stand inside a circle with one foot out, and someone throws a tennis ball in the middle of the circle (see image).

The player whose foot is hit by the ball has to go and bring back the packet with the potatoes, guessing from all the packets. The player must check the packets one after another until they determine which is the potato packet. If the player doesn't bring back the potato packet, the other players will tease them, and they must go back and choose again. When they finally bring back the one with the potatoes, the packets are sorted again. Once again, the tennis ball is thrown, another player is chosen, and the game continues.

85. Dori-laaf or Bet-laaf (Jumping Rope)

Jumping rope is a form of exercise, and it is very common among people of all ages. It is a beneficial way to lose fat and stay healthy, and doctors often advise patients to include this in their daily fitness routine. However, in Bangladesh, jumping rope is also a competitive game, and it is especially popular among young girls in rural villages. The game is even a part of school sports competitions in some villages and towns.

Only one length of rope per player is required for this game. However, it can't be just any rope; it must be durable, that is, strong, heavy, well-twisted, and stiff. It should be comparable to the thick and robust cow rope used in the villages in Bangladesh. In fact, in the past, girls in the villages used to collect rope used for tying cows or goats for the game. However, as jump ropes are available in stores now, the trend of using cow rope has decreased.

During the winter season, girls compete against each other and also enjoy warming up in the cold weather in a fun way. Often, to make the game more challenging, two girls rotate a long rope, and one or more other players jump over it in unison. Sometimes even young boys join in the game to try to beat the girls, and the competition becomes more intense because it is boys versus girls.

Jumping rope used to be an everyday scene throughout Bangladesh. Girls in the villages could be seen playing outside in groups, filling the cold winter mornings and evenings with laughter and liveliness. Nowadays, however, this isn't seen as much anymore.

86. Laatim Khela (Spinning a Top)

The *Laatim* game is quite popular in Bangladesh as are similar games played with tops worldwide. Yards or open spaces with flat surfaces are the most suitable places to play this type of game. In South Asia, kids play it more often during winter days. A toy called a *laatim* is needed to play this game. There are many types of *laatim*, and the game can be played in many different ways.

A *laatim* is a round-shaped cone-like object made of wood, similar to a spinning top (see image). The shape is similar to that of a guava fruit. A metal spike in the center goes from one end of the wooden object to the other and sticks out through the narrow end, like a nail. One has to wrap a jute cord around the body of the *laatim* and then throw it on the ground with a certain technique, keeping the cord end in one hand. The cord unwraps, and the *laatim* starts spinning on the ground. It may also move across the ground while spinning. The size of the metal and rope needed depends on the size and shape of the *laatim*. Not everyone can spin a *laatim* properly. It needs a lot of practice, just like a yo-yo.

Although there are many ways to play with a *laatim*, we will only discuss two ways here. The first way is that the kids will simply throw their *laatim* to the ground and make it spin. Whoever can make it spin the longest is the winner. The other way is that the kids first draw a circle (or any other shape) on the ground, and then the players throw down their *laatim*, trying to keep them spinning within the marked space. If a *laatim* leaves the marked space before it stops spinning, it will be counted as an "out," and that player will be dismissed from the game.

Chapter 3: Outdoor Games Played in Trees or Ponds

87. Gaachooya Gaachooya Khela (Game of Tag Played in Trees)

Village boys and shepherds typically play the *Gaachooya Gaachooya* game. Although it is a team game, players also need to compete against each other in some ways. Usually, a garden with many big trees like mango trees or lychee trees is a suitable place to play. The big trees provide great cover for the players to hide themselves. Only a single stick is needed to play it.

To play, one of the players is selected to be the *chor* (thief). The thief stands in a circle with a stick that is touching their feet, showing their possession of the stick. The other players go up in or hide under the trees where the thief won't be able to touch them without needing to leave the circle. The thief is only allowed to leave the circle if they leave their stick behind there. The players try to tempt the thief to leave the circle so they can steal the thief's stick. The thief's goal is to leave the circle, tag a player, and then return quickly before the stick is taken. If the thief succeeds in tagging a player and returning to the circle to take possession of the stick, the thief wins, and the player they tagged will be the next thief. But if one of the other players can take possession of the stick while the thief is out of the circle, the thief loses.

The game's prevalence can be seen especially in the Mymensingh district. In Murshidabad, it is known as *Sholjhaapta Khela*. There, instead of sticks, one can touch tree trunks. In the

Bikrampur district, it is known as *Dogaare Chog* and is played in a slightly modified form.

The main goal of the game is the joy of rampaging around and playing in the trees. There is no use of force or strength required for it. The only required skill is the agility to climb up and down a tree with speed and stamina. Playing in the trees reflects living life in the wild.

In *Gaachooya Gaachooya* there is also a rhyme, which goes like this:

> *Gaachooya re Gaachooya*
> Why are you in the tree?
> Out of the fear of the tiger.
> Where is the tiger?
> On the ground.
> Where is the ground?
> Here it is.
> How many brothers do you have?
> Seven brothers.
> Will you give me one brother?
> Only if you can touch him.

There is another game from Murshidabad called *Soljhaapta* (Kissing the Stick), which is similar to the *Gaachooya Gaachooya* game. *Soljhaapta* is usually played by cowherds in mango or litchi orchards.

First, the thief is chosen by a coin toss. Then, the thief places a stick on the ground and stands nearby, touching one side of it, while the other players climb up nearby trees. The thief must tag one of the players up in a tree and then rush back to the stick and kiss it. If the thief succeeds, the player that was tagged becomes the thief in the next round. To avoid losing, the player who was tagged must jump down from the tree and take the thief's stick away without getting caught while another player tries to distract the thief. Also, tagging the player only counts when they are in the tree, and only the player who was tagged may try to take away the stick. The thief can also tag someone else while the tagged one is trying to take the stick. So, the challenge for the other players is to not get tagged while in a tree. Also, players are not allowed to climb so high that they are completely out of the thief's reach.

88. Kola Gaacher Dolna (Banana Tree Merry-Go-Round)

This game is similar to riding a merry-go-round. To begin, a banana tree trunk 2-3 feet in length is cut. Then, it is buried in the ground standing straight up, keeping about half of it above ground. A hard piece of tree branch about 1-2 feet in length is pierced into the top of the trunk. Next, a full-size banana tree, which is normally 6-10 feet long, is centered on top of the trunk, parallel to the ground, and pierced by the hard piece of tree branch (see image). When the ride is complete, two kids sit on either end of the longer piece. Other kids push the ends of the longer piece to make the ride rotate. This is a lot of fun for the kids sitting on it, and the kids take turns riding and pushing.

89. Pichhil Kola Gaache Chora (Climb the Slippery Banana Tree)

To play this game, a banana tree is made slippery by peeling off two to four of its upper layers, making climbing it very difficult. The peels are then placed in a hole in the ground. Though it is typically a children's game, adults can also participate as it is a game of strength and strategy. Whoever manages to climb to the top of the tree wins.

90. Baalish Khela (Pillow Fight Game)

This is a very interesting game of strategy and strength. First, a narrow bridge *(shaako)* is built from bamboo, having a width of no more than a few inches (see image). Two players stand on the bridge and, while keeping their balance, have to hit the other with a pillow and try to make them fall off the bridge. Players swing a pillow with one hand and block their opponent's hits with the other. Whoever can throw the other off the bridge first wins. There are referees and judges for the game to check if the players are cheating and help avoid foul play. The ground under the bridge is soft, so players won't get injured after falling. This game is more or less familiar all over Bangladesh.

91. Paata Chena Khela (Leaf Identifying Game)

Paata Chena Khela is a game that tests how many trees the players can identify by looking at leaves. To begin, all players hide, and an adult collects some tree leaves. After they are done collecting, they signal the players to come out. Then, the adult takes the leaves one by one and asks the players individually to say the name of the tree that the leaves belong to. The adult only reveals the right answer when everyone's turn is completed. Whoever can say the most tree names correctly wins the game. The players also say a rhyme about leaves at the end of the game.

This game is educational for children as it helps them learn about nature. Recognizing plants is crucial for villagers because different types of leaves have different purposes such as *aayoorveda* (an alternative medicine system used throughout the Indian subcontinent) and different types of worship or religious rituals. Parents introduce important plants to their children through this game.

92. Paanir Moddhe Polo Khela (Water Polo Game)

Paanir Moddhe Polo Khela is the traditional "Water Polo" game. Unlike the regular polo game, which is played on horseback, this game is played in water. Water polo was created after the polo game gained recognition.

Polo was initially known as *Poolu*, and it was called *Chovgan* or *Chowgan* in ancient Persia. It was also common in ancient China. Sultan Qutb ud-Din Aibak died after falling from his horse while playing polo in the thirteenth century. Akbar the Great was also a fan of polo. In the second Olympic Games in 1900, polo was included for the first time. It was during this time that the game of water polo gained popularity.

Water polo is usually played in a swimming pool or lake. Before starting a game, the game boundaries and goalposts are marked. Each team has seven players who play the game while swimming. Players throw around a light ball that floats on water with their hands to try to score a goal. The game is overseen by a referee who is usually on a nearby boat or alongside the pool

93. Koya-Koyi Khela (Water Hyacinth Game)

Koya-Koyi can be played in ponds or swimming pools where the water is about chest-deep. In Bangladesh, village children play this game together in ponds or rivers. They usually use the tip of a water hyacinth about two inches long for the game. If they can't get a water hyacinth, they can use a plastic pipe or toy as an alternative, as long as it floats in the water so they won't lose it.

A player starts the game by spitting out water either using the water hyacinth as a funnel or directly from their mouth. They either have to fill the water hyacinth or their mouth with water and then spit it out on others (see image). After the first player initiates, others randomly splash water toward each other with their hands.

While playing and splashing water, if anyone ends up touching the water hyacinth or the toy/pipe, the person who initiated *Koya-Koyi* has to dive underwater. But if someone touches this person before they can dive, then that player wins. So, the one with the water hyacinth must dive underwater with the water hyacinth/pipe/toy before anyone can reach and touch them. The winner initiates a new game by spitting water through the water hyacinth or toy pipe, and the game continues. The game is mostly played in the Magura, Jessore, and Narail districts.

Sometimes children play with mud while playing in the water, and they throw mud at each other instead of water. This version is called *Kaada Paakkapaakki Khela.*

94. Haari Baaich Khela (Cooking Pot Game)

This is a racing game on the water, but unlike *Nouka Baaich* (Boat Race, see Part III), it is a single-player race instead of a team sport. In rural Bangladesh, farmers have big cooking pots on hand for different agricultural purposes. For example, to make rice out of paddy, they need to boil the paddy in giant pots. Also, to make molasses or raw sugar from date syrup, farmers use big pots.

Kids, usually six to twelve years old, take these big pots to the ponds, sit inside the pot, and race each other. They use their hands instead of oars to paddle. Two, three, or even ten kids participate in this game and try to cross the pond. Whoever reaches the other side first wins the game.

95. Laai or Joloi Khela (Diving Underwater Game)

Laai or *Joloi Khela* is mainly played by boys while swimming and diving in ponds or lakes. The word *laai* comes from the word for "navel" (pronounced "navi" in Bengali), as the goal of the game is to reach navel-deep (waist-deep) water. *Laai* is also mentioned in love songs and athletic lyrics in rural areas. The word *joloi* comes from the Bangla word *jol*, meaning "water." Besides *Laai* and *Joloi*, this game has another name, *Doob diye maach dhora* (dipping and fishing). It is mostly played in the Comilla, Dhaka, and Mymensingh districts. Muhammad Sirajuddin Kasimpuri once wrote about this game:

To begin, one player, standing chest-deep in the water, takes some water in the palm of his hand and asks the others:

Aamar haate kee? (What's in my hand?)

Joloi. (Water.)

Ek doobe taai tore jodi paai (If I catch you with one dive)

Ek gerashe khai. (I will devour you in one gulp.)

Reciting this, he tries to swim underwater to get to a place with navel-deep water while the others try to catch him underwater before he gets there. He wins if he manages to reach there without getting caught and says *"Aanga Aanga"* immediately after coming out of the water. He loses if he gets caught before arriving there or doesn't say the words.

The other boys also take turns one by one, after saying the rhyme again. The boy whose turn it is can also choose to float a distance before diving underwater. But the others can only catch him when he is underwater. Catching him while he is floating doesn't count.

Another version of this game goes by the name *Holdoog* and is played by boys while they are bathing in rivers or ponds. One boy is chosen to be "It" through a coin toss. This boy begins the game by taking some water in his hand and asking questions for the others to answer.

> The boy asks, pointing to his hand: *Eta kee?* (What is this?)
>
> Other boys: *Doodh.* (Milk.)
>
> The boy drops the water and takes some more in his cupped hands.
>
> He asks again: *Eta kee?* (What is this?)
>
> Others: *Tyal.* (Oil.)
>
> The boy continues to ask the question again in the same way.
>
> Others: Morich. (Chili.)
>
> Then the boy says the last line, rhyming with the previous answer.
>
> *Baap bole dhoris!* (Catch it if you can!)

As soon as the boy finishes the rhyme, he dives underwater, and the other boys try to find him. The one who touches him first becomes the next boy to question the others in the next round.

The game is known as *Maalai* in Mymensingh and *Haattihaatti* in Noakhali.

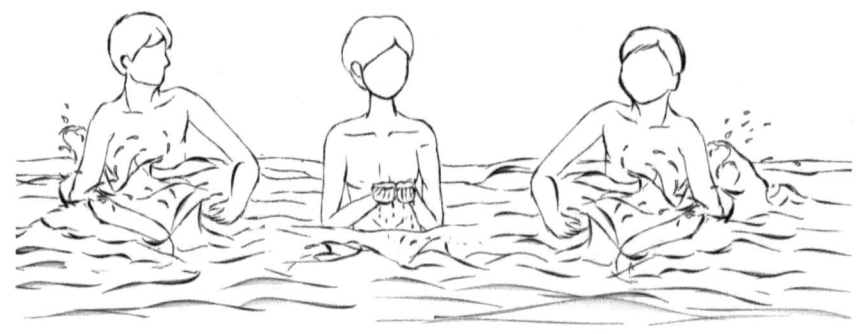

96. Kaada Paakkapaakki Khela (Catch the Mud Game)

Children and teenagers in the villages love to play with mud and water while bathing in rivers or ponds. *Kaada Paakkapaakki Khela* is both a competitive sport and a favorite bathtime game.

To play, the first player scoops up some mud and throws it as far as they can over the water, beginning to say a rhyme. Everyone else starts swimming towards where the mud lands. The goal is to swim fast enough to catch some of the mud before it dissolves in the water. Whoever manages to catch it first is the winner.

The rhyme for this game is as follows:

First Player: *Eidaa kee?* (What is it?)

Everyone: *Kaada.* (It is mud.)

First Player: *Oi taamaat je na jaaibe shey ekta gaadha!* (Whoever can't reach there and catch the mud is a fool!)

Another version of this game is called *Jhaapoori Khela. Jhaapoori* means "the one who is doing the *jhaap* (jump)." In this case, the term usually refers to jumping around in the water and making a big splash/noise. To play, the players (usually boys) all stand in waist-deep water in a pond and form a circle. One of them holds a fruit that can float on the water. He throws the fruit up, and everybody rushes to catch it as it comes back down. The game is also known as *Taai Taai Khela* (Clap Clap Game) in some regions.

97. Bang Laafaano Khela (Frog Jumping Game)

This is another water game that is very popular among boys. This game is usually played in the shallow water near the banks of a lake, pond, or calm river. It is very pleasant and heartwarming to see boys merrily playing and jumping in the water together. A *chaara* (a small flat stone or hardened clay piece) is the main prop required to play this game. Players throw a *chaara* over the water as far as they can, like skipping a rock. While the *chaara* is still moving forward, the player has to dive into the water and come up again, like a frog, as many times as possible. Other players count how many jumps that player can make with one *chaara's* journey. The player who makes the most jumps wins. This continuous jumping in the water inspired the game's name, the Frog Jumping Game.

Players often sing rhymes while playing. The content of the rhyme is about frogs.

98. Brishtir Jonno Khela (Rain Game)

There was a traditional belief that the rain would come faster if people got wet and rolled themselves in water and clay. Therefore, people used to do this to invoke rain during a drought.

In the spring or during the months of *Faalgoon-Chaitro-Boishaakh* (roughly, March-May), when the whole country was on the verge of burning up from the heat and being destroyed by drought, the village children went in groups from house to house, reciting this rhyme. The people in the houses would pour water on them, and they would roll in the yard, hoping rain would come soon.

These days, people only play it as a fun game to preserve this tradition. Kids say various rhymes while playing this game, which may differ depending on the region. One of the most popular rhymes is given below:

Aay brishti jhepe. (Come, oh rain! Pour down heavily!)

Dhaan debo mepe. (We will offer rice in plenty.)

Leboor paatay koromchaa. (Natal plum is on lime leaves.)

Jaa brishti jhore jaa! (Oh rain! Go on! Keep on pouring down!)

Another version of this game goes by the name *Kaadamaati Khela* (Clay Game), with the same gameplay but different rhymes.

The rhyme for this game goes like this:

Tetool beechi pekhom dhor. (Hold the tamarind seed and hold onto your wings.)

Gooroom gooroom baadol jhor. (Oh rain! Pour down making the sound *"gooroom gooroom."*)

Faata aashmaan! Chilaiyya de! (With your rain, crack open the sky! Peel it off!)

Chapter 4: Outdoor Acting Games and Role Plays

99. Koomir Koomi Khela (Crocodile Crocodile Game)

In the evenings, it is a common scene in rural villages to see children merrily playing *Koomir Koomi Khela*, an interesting story of a mother crocodile and her eggs. There is no fixed number of players required for this game, and it is best played in an area where the ground is higher in one spot than another. This way, the lower area can be used as the *nodi* (river) and the higher one as the *teer* (shore).

To begin, one player is selected to play the mother crocodile, and this player goes down to the river area with her make-believe eggs. A few of the other players walk down to the river area from the shore. They crouch down, pretending they are bathing and submerged in the water. They move their hands and legs around to pretend they are swimming, taking deep breaths while going in and out of the water.

They recite this verse:

> *Koomir, tomaar paanite naamchi.* (Hey, crocodile! We got in your water.)

Hearing that, the crocodile chases, and the players immediately go up to the shore area. When the players are on the shore, they are safe, since the crocodile can't leave the water. The players' goal is to make the crocodile abandon her eggs and chase the persons who had gotten into the water while the remaining players go to the crocodile's den, a bit far from the shore, and eat her eggs. When she sees that, the mother crocodile becomes even more angry and now chases after the group eating her eggs. If anyone gets caught, they become the crocodile in the next round, and the former crocodile gets to join the other players. And as such, the game continues. The players may also say rhymes while playing the game.

100. Chaagol Dhora Khela (Goat Catching Game)

Chaagol Dhora Khela is a popular game of make-believe where children act out the story of catching a goat. To begin, players make a circle, holding hands with each other, and one player stands in the middle of the circle, playing the goat. Two players stand outside the circle and play the goat's owner and a landowner (see image).

The circle made by the rest of the players becomes the landowner's chili field, where the goat has just barged in. The goat then pretends to eat the chilis in the chili field. Seeing that, the landowner shouts at the goat saying, "Argh! The goat is eating all my chili! Who in the world's goat is that? Get it off my field!"

But the goat owner doesn't respond and pretends that the goat isn't his. So, the landowner interrogates the goat owner about what his goat typically eats and tricks him into saying what it looks like.

After confirming that the goat in question indeed belongs to the goat owner, the landowner threatens the goat. He runs to chase the goat, and the goat's owner also runs after the goat. The goat leaves the circle and runs away from both of them. Whichever of the two is able to catch the goat first becomes the goat in the next round.

101. Baagh-Baagh Khela (Tiger-Tiger Game)

Baagh-Baagh Khela is another popular game of make-believe where children act like they are trying to save themselves from a tiger. One player becomes the tiger and stands in a circle, usually drawn near a tree. The other children sit on the branches of the tree. Then, a conversation starts among them; the tiger asks them questions, and they answer. The tiger tries to trick them into lowering their guard and climbing down from the tree. Eventually, the players act like they got tricked and climb down, and the tiger immediately attacks them. The first person to get caught by the tiger becomes the tiger in the next round. The tiger can also climb the tree to try to catch the players. However, if the tiger needs to leave the circle to do that and one of the players jumps down into the circle before the tiger is able to catch anyone, the tiger loses, and the game restarts with the same person being the tiger again.

102. Ayanga-Ayanga (The Tiger and the Goats Game)

This game is played in a group by both boys and girls. To begin, a large circle is drawn on the ground. One player plays the role of the tiger and remains outside the circle while the other players play the goats and stand inside it. The tiger recites different rhymes and goes around the circle, trying to catch the goats off guard.

One such rhyme used in the game in the Jessore region goes as follows:

> Tiger: *Waa waa!* (Mimicking the sound of crying)
>
> Goats (in chorus): *Kaandosh ken?* (What are you crying for?)
>
> Tiger: *Goru haaraichi!* (I lost a cow!)
>
> Goats: *Kemon goru?* (What sort of cow?)
>
> Tiger: *Laal goru.* (A red one.)
>
> Goats: *Shing aache?* (Does it have horns?)
>
> Tiger: *Ho.* (Yes.)
>
> Goats: *Ekta gaan ko.* (Sing a song.)

The tiger then begins to dance around while singing, "Who took my cow? Who took my cow? Come here, whoever took my cow." Suddenly, the tiger stops and jumps forward to drag one of the goats out of the circle. The other players try to hold onto the goat so that the tiger cannot take them away.

The tiger may only capture one goat at a time and can only jump once inside the circle to drag the targeted player out. Once the victim is dragged out of the circle's boundary, they will be considered captured. The goats taken out of the circle by the tiger stay on the tiger's side.

The last player remaining in the circle becomes the tiger in the next round.

103. Koitor Baaccha Khela (Baby Pigeon Game)

A baby pigeon is called *koitor baaccha* in the Chittagong district, and this game is well-known in that area. Young girls and boys play the game together, acting out a story where they buy items from a peddler.

At the beginning of the game, 10 to 15 children stand behind each other, forming a long line. The player at the very front of the line becomes the *koitor*, or the mother pigeon. All of the children behind her are *koitor baaccha*, or baby pigeons.

Another player remains outside of this line and plays the role of *paashaari*, or the peddler. They have a bag over their shoulder and a branch on their head.

Paashaari shouts this rhyme to sell their wares:
Ke kee neebi? (Anyone want to buy something?)
Shob Jeenish aache! (I have all kinds of things here!)

When the other players hear the rhyme, all of the baby pigeons respond, and a conversation begins.

> Pigeons: *Cheerooni aache?* (Do you have a comb?)
>
> Peddler: *Aache.* (Yes.)
>
> Pigeons: *Aamra cheerooni nebo, daam koto?* (We will take the comb. How much is it?)
>
> Peddler: *Paach taaka.* (Five *taaka*). Note: Since this game is very old, the monetary value for the same amount of Bangladeshi *taaka* (BDT) now would be around 20 *taaka* or 20 cents BDT (17 cents USD).
>
> Pigeons: *Daam beshi, nebonaa.* (The price is too high; we won't take it.)

The peddler then turns to leave and sell their products somewhere else. But seeing the peddler go, the baby pigeons call out again, and the peddler comes back. The baby pigeons ask to buy a comb again, and the bargaining resumes.

But when the peddler still refuses to lower the price, the babies start crying. The mother pigeon finally gives in to their demands and agrees to buy the comb for them. She asks the peddler to accept her payment the next time the peddler comes through town because she doesn't have the money with her at the moment.

The peddler agrees and leaves. After getting the make-believe comb, the baby pigeons pretend to start brushing their hair one by one, starting from the first one in line to the end of the line. When the last baby begins to brush their hair, the comb breaks. Feeling angry, they throw it into the river.

When the peddler returns, the baby pigeons complain that the comb was defective, so they will not pay any money. Hearing this, the peddler gets angry and tells the mother that if she doesn't pay the money, the peddler will kidnap one of the babies.

But before the mother can say anything, the babies start running away out of fear, and the peddler runs after them to catch them. The game ends when the peddler catches a baby pigeon. The player that gets caught becomes the peddler in the next round.

104. Aanchaabaati/Topabhaati (Playing House Game)

In the *Aanchaabaati* or *Topabhaati* game, young children pretend to be adults and mimic adult domestic chores and activities. *Aanchaa* means coconut shell, and *baati* means a pot, so "*aanchaabaati*" refers to a pot made from a coconut shell. *Topa* means a pot made of clay, and *bhaati* comes from the word *bhaat*, meaning rice, so "*topabhaati*" means cooking rice in a crock. These terms both refer to cooking rice, a basic everyday task in the villagers' life. As such, cooking rice represents the domestic life of villagers, as does this game, which is how the game's name came to be.

Both girls and boys participate in this game as it includes many aspects of daily life, from preparing a playhouse to mimicking cooking. This game also exhibits children's creative skills and knowledge of domestic life responsibilities. For villagers, homemaking is considered a very crucial skill. Therefore, the children who are better at playing this game are acknowledged as brilliant individuals.

To begin the game, the children build playhouses using their creativity. The poles of the houses are made of bamboo twigs. The roof is comprised of coconut leaves, betel nuts, or leaves from other plants. Mud or clay is used to plaster the walls. Besides these materials, children collect abandoned items and anything they can find to use as play tools. For example, empty cans, discarded paper products, old bottles, broken plates, or glassware are used. They make a toy stove out of clay, which is a smaller version of the real one called *aalochoola*. Sometimes, the stove is made from three bricks or lumps of bricks. The children collect hard coconut shells known as *aanchaa* or *maala* as cooking utensils. A pan is made by sanding the corners of a broken crock. Sand or rice dust is used as an alternative to rice. Sometimes, the game is played with crumbled rice pieces, known as *khood*. Taro and jackfruit leaves are used as plates.

After preparing all the materials, one player plays as the head male figure of the usual patriarchal village family and goes into the woods to pretend to shop. Shopping bags are made with areca, banana, or date palm leaves. They come back with some bushes as vegetables and wild fruits as fish. They act exhausted from shopping and drop the bags inside the pretend kitchen with a sigh. The players playing housewives and daughters quickly come forward, grab the bags, and prepare to cook. The cooking part is very enjoyable for the younger children. They pretend as if they are preparing a feast. They carefully cut the ingredients as if they were experienced chefs. They pretend to light a cooking a fire like an expert villager by blowing on the smoke. Sometimes, children roll their hands over their eyes, pretending to shed tears from the smoke.

After finishing the cooking, the players eat. The cooks do not eat right away. Rather, they serve the master of the house, who is usually the husband, first. The food is presented to the husband and elders of the family like in any common household in the village. Dishes are served on the leaves of different trees, and the children always pretend to eat with great satisfaction. They also don't forget to praise the cooks for the delicious food, to the delight of the children playing the cooks.

After everyone is done eating, they pretend it is nighttime and go to sleep. They lie down on the ground and begin to snore. Some additional details are added; for example, some may wake up suddenly as if there were loud sounds, or some will lie down and toss and turn. The game ends with everyone finally sleeping.

The adults laugh as they watch the children act hilariously. Sometimes, they feel nostalgic watching the kids playing house, remembering their childhood. They may also feel sad thinking about how the game of playing house is fun and amusing, unlike the struggles and stress of real domestic life.

There is even a well-known expression that goes, "This is not an *Aanchaabaati* game that I can play whenever I want and stop whenever I don't want to anymore." This verse is mostly used in the context of marriage, which is neither a kid's game that can be stopped anytime nor something done just for fun. However, this game can be useful because children learn how to adapt to everyday domestic life, manage a household, and follow the rules regarding respecting their elders and others. As such, this game can also be called the "school of adult family life."

105. Maachdhora Khela (Fishing Game)

Maachdhora Khela is a game where children pretend to catch fish. The playing equipment includes a fishing rod, a fish-keeping pot, a fish creel (basket), and several chairs. Curiously, the most common tool for catching fish, a net, is not used in this game.

Children position themselves to catch fish on a make-believe pond or river. Some locals believe in a God of the river named *Dhaamaalya*. They worship him and pray for catching a lot of fish while fishing. Children imitate this practice in the game. They also recite a rhyme which asks for a great catch.

The next part of the game is played similarly to the *Chair e Bosha* (Sitting in a Chair) game—see Part I, Chapter 2. Several chairs are placed for the players to sit while fishing. However, there is one less chair than the total number of players. Each round, after the rhyme is said, players must quickly stand up from their seats and run to another. Whoever fails to occupy a new seat gets dismissed from the game. After each round, one chair is removed, and the game is played similarly again. The game continues until one player is left sitting, and this person is the winner.

Part III:
Competitions and Festival Games

In addition to the many outdoor games of Bangladesh, there are some games that are for special occasions like festivals, competitions, and sports events. In this part, we show some of the most common celebratory and competitive games in Bangladesh that are enjoyed by children and adults alike.

Chapter 1: Racing Games and Competitions

106. Tin Paaye Dour (Three-Legged Race)

Tin Paaye Dour is a running race usually held at annual school and college sporting competitions. This game is basically a foot race that is run in teams of two where the teammates' legs are tied together with a towel—one's partner's right leg to the other's left leg (see image). In this situation, the two players must work as a unit and race against other teams to a certain point. Many teams can participate in this game. Referees and judges are also required. First, second, and third prizes are given to the winning pairs, and the prizes also come in pairs, one for each teammate.

107. Baadha-bighner Dour (Obstacle Course Race)

Baadha-bighner Dour is another running competition, but the contestants run while facing obstacles along the way. Different types of objects are placed on the running path so that participants have to jump or swiftly change direction to avoid them while running.

To begin, all players stand near the starting line. With the referee's first whistle, each player takes their position at the line. After the second whistle, everyone starts running at once. Those who can reach the endpoint (finish line) and successfully avoid all the hurdles per the organizers' instructions will be awarded 1st, 2nd, and 3rd place, respectively. This is a game of acrobatics, strength, and strategy.

Raju Mahajan

108. Biscuit Dour (Biscuit Race)

Biscuit Dour is also another running competition that is usually part of a school's annual or other periodic sports competition. This game is played in different regions with slight variations in the rules.

At one end of the running field, participants take their positions at the starting line with their hands tied behind their backs. On the other side of the field, biscuits are hung on strings from a horizontal pole, leaving a small distance between each biscuit. The biscuits are also hung a little higher than the players' reach so that the runners will have to jump up to get them (see image).

Because the players' hands are tied, they can only use their mouths to grab the biscuit. They can either take the whole biscuit in their mouth and pull it down or break the string and take both the biscuit and the string. Both methods are allowed. However, if the biscuit falls from the runner's mouth or off of the string while the player is trying to get it down, that person will be disqualified from the game.

In some competitions, there is one biscuit assigned to each participant, and they are hung in front of each person's specific running line or mark. The players run on their marks, and whoever manages to get to the target area, snatch their biscuit, and return to the start first wins. In this variation, three winners are awarded.

In another variation of this competition, there are more biscuits than competitors hung to allow the players more than one chance at taking a biscuit if one happens to fall.

In yet another variation, there is only one biscuit hung per competitor, however, players are allowed to take more than one biscuit, which creates a greater challenge for the other players. Some children even risk their chance of winning only for the fun of taking away other players' biscuits. However, this rule is usually allowed only in a more casual setting, such as at a school picnic or other such occasion when the game is only played for fun. Children really love this game.

109. Ongko Dour (Math Race)

Ongko Dour is similar to the Biscuit Race and is often played at annual school or college sports competitions. Three winners are also chosen in this game.

However, instead of snatching a biscuit, participants have to solve a math problem and then run back to their starting place. A participant will only be declared the winner if they solved the question correctly.

Unlike *Biscuit Dour*, *Ongko Dour* is more challenging and usually played by teenagers. In this game, the participants have to remain calm and level-headed in order to resolve the math problems quickly and correctly. But at the same time, they need to be very fast on their feet. Nevertheless, this type of game is a positive motivation for the students to be good at math.

110. Shaatar Khela (Swimming Race)

Shaatar Khela is a swimming game played by village children, usually in rivers or canals big enough for racing. The players employ different ways of swimming, for example, *doob shaatar* (swimming while being completely underwater) and *ooltaa shaatar* (swimming backwards) to challenge each other.

111. Nouka Baaich (Boat Race)

Nouka Baaich (Boat Race) is one of the most popular games in Bangladesh and is very similar to an American or European-style boat race. Because Bangladesh is a riverine country (more than 230 rivers and the world's largest delta), rivers have an immense influence on Bengali economic, social, and cultural life. A boat is more than just a means of transport. The life and livelihood of so many boatmen, fishermen, and sailors are intimately connected to boats. Others use boats as entertainment centers and even as homes. Boats in Bangladesh are treated as a symbol of the livelihood of the common people, and they play an important role in the region's cultural history.

As such, *Nouka Baaich* is an ancient and traditional folk game that reflects the history of Bengali culture. It is also a game of endurance and agility as the boats used in the race do not have masts or sails and must be rowed by the participants. Therefore, the strength and strategy of the rowers and helmsmen are deciding factors in this game, which is often played competitively during fairs and *Poojas* (Hindu festivals). While the race goes on through one or two miles of a river, people of all ages sit on boats and trees along the riverbank to watch and have as much fun as the participants.

The race takes on a festive vibe when the crowd sings special songs with rhymes (called *shaarigaans*) composed only for the *Nouka Baaich* game. As the young men row with determination to win the race, musicians beat drums and play other percussion instruments, and the audience sings enticing songs in chorus. Other than drums, instruments such as a *dotaara* (a two-stringed instrument) and a *sharinda* are also commonly used, and the singer and the chorus sing together, sometimes sitting in or standing on a boat. Young girls wearing red or yellow dresses wave handkerchiefs and dance harmoniously together. The rhythmic sound from their jangling anklets creates an amazing cadence, mixing with the sound of waves in the river. The race gets intense as the rowers keep thrashing their oars fiercely in the water in harmony with the raging beats of the songs and music.

The racing boats are usually forty to sixty feet long and five to six feet wide. At dawn on race day, villagers blow the horn, and, when the drum roll sounds, the race participants arrive at the venue. The participants prepare their boats for the race from dawn until noon by rubbing tar, bananas, and flour on them. The materials make the boat's body so slippery that, as soon as the boat is in the river, a little push is all it takes for it to glide fast and smoothly through the water.

Even though boat races are mostly done only on special occasions, these are not the only times this game is played. They can also be done recreationally or solely for entertainment. For example, in the Hindu community, on the first day of the Bengali month of *Bhaadro,* they always arrange boat races as a part of the *Monaasha Pooja*; however, the race itself has no historical connection with the *pooja*. The race only adds to the festive, joyous environment. Although the boat race has been run every year for decades on this day in the Pirojpur and Najirpur sub-districts, it is now done on this occasion across the country.

Organization of the Race:

To organize the race peacefully, the villagers set up a committee beforehand to decide and instruct on how the race will be run. Before the race starts, the committee places two red flags in the ground to mark the beginning point of the race. Participants will row from there until they reach a certain point which is the finish line. The committee then places two green flags on a raft at the finish line. Whichever boat makes it to the finish line's green flag from the starting point's red flag first is the winner.

It is undeniable that in this game, the strength of the oars and how the participants hold their oars are crucial in terms of winning. For this, the boatmen and other participants need to be synchronized and disciplined with each other. Once all forty to fifty boats of the race gather to compete, two boats of the same size are paired to race each other. Both boats start the race simultaneously. Whichever boat reaches the green flag first wins, and the participation of those two boats finishes there. The boat race has some other rules as well, and anyone who violates those rules is excluded from the game. The people who participate in the boat race are usually from a Hindu or Muslim community, and some of them are elite people from the village. The viewers can be people of all ages.

Those who row the oars are known as *baacheledaar*. They sit on both sides of the boat and row in sync. *Shaaridaar* sing while standing in the middle of the boat's platform. The number of *baacheledaar* and *shaaridaar* can be anywhere from 7 to 100 and range in age from 20 to 50+ years old. As mentioned, boats do not have masts or sails, and motor engines are also not allowed. On the day of the race, the boat is decorated with the *aalpona* (artwork of different designs or mandalas) using rice flour and vermilion. It is done on the outer body and platform of the boat. Since it is a competition on the water, the participants wear tight-fitting clothes to reduce the possibility of accidents.

Boat racing is primarily an activity for wealthy people. From making the boat to coloring and decorating the body of the boat, a racing boat costs around one *laac* (roughly $1,100 USD/€1,000). On top of that, the entertainment, feast, and fees of the rowers and *shaaridaar* on the day of the competition all cost a lot of money.

In the past, during the race, teams tried to push the competitor's boat off course and get it stuck on a *chhor*, a large deposit of sand and dirt that looks like an island when the tide is low. Then they would row past the competitor before they could escape from the *chhor* and win the race. They also cheated by making holes in the deck of the competitor's boat before the start of the race to make them take in water and lose. Sometimes, these actions would lead to fights among the participants, and many would be wounded or injured.

History of Nouka Baaich:

Nouka Baaich is a very old tradition of the folk Bengali culture going back centuries, possibly to medieval times when Muslim landlords also arranged boat races. In those times in East Bengal, the naval force was one of the most important ways to defend and conquer the kingdoms. In the sixteenth century, the Baro-Bhuiyans of Bengal went up against the naval force of the Mughals. The victory in the fight mostly depended on the agility and the strategy of the crewmen. On the battleships, there used to be long-shaped rod boats. These rod boats are still useful for boat races. In their leisure time, the navy also organized races in their festivals. Eventually, the feudal era ended, and this naval force was extinguished. However, the culture and rituals of such races survived through the creation of the game of *Nouka Baaich*.

112. Baaichaali Khela (Racing on Bamboo Raft Game)

Baaichaali Khela is another racing game on the water. However, instead of a boat, a *bhela* (a small platform created by tying bamboo together) is used (see image). Each participant races individually with their *bhela*. During the rainy season, when the fields are submerged in water, the excitement of playing *Baaichaali* elates the village children. The boys cut big banana trees to prepare their *bhela* and then test to see if they will float on the water. Everything from making the *bhela* to seeing boys competing in groups is a stunning scene. Rhymes are recited during the contest as well. Although the game can be seen in different parts of Bangladesh, it is prevalent in the Mymensingh and Barisal districts.

113. Daaria Baandha (Stealing the Salt Game)

Daaria Baandha is the most popular game in rural areas of Bangladesh. It is played by drawing a specific diagram on a large area of open ground. Anyone can participate in this game, even the elders. There is an obligatory boundary in the game. On winter afternoons, kids in the village get really excited about this game and play *Daaria Baandha* in great numbers.

In order to play *Daaria Baandha*, you must have a large area of fallow land, that is, an area of farmland that is not currently being cultivated. The fallow parcel of land is then converted into a play area by drawing a court. This game has little appeal in urban areas, as there is a severe shortage of fallow land in these areas.

In spite of its immense popularity, there is no federation for *Daaria Baandha* in Bangladesh. Yet sports such as soccer, billiards, squash, and weightlifting—whose identity and popularity are limited to a small number of people—have federations. On the other hand, *Daaria Baandha* is a very popular game in rural communities, and with the formation of a federation, this game could spread rapidly and become popular with children across the country.

There is considerable disagreement regarding the origin of the *Daaria Baandha* game. However, it can be said that this game has been played since ancient times. And because there is no governing federation, there are also no specific rules and regulations for this game.

This game is played between two teams of five to seven players, each in a large square marked out on the ground (see image). Depending on how many players there are, several smaller squares (or cells) are drawn inside the large one. One of the smaller squares is called *godighor* (team's chamber) and another is called *lobonghor* (salt chamber). The members of one team (Team A) must go inside the *godighor* at the beginning of the game while the opposing team's members (Team B) arrange themselves so that no one from Team A can move from one square to another. A member of Team A then tries to leave the *godighor*, move through every cell, and make their way back to the *godighor* by darting back and forth to avoid the Team B players, who are on guard. A team earns points and wins the round if one of its members can cross every square without getting touched by the other team. But this team loses the round if their player is touched by one of the opposition's players. At the end of the round, the opposing team takes the field and does the same. The winning team is determined by adding up the points that each team has accrued throughout the game.

114. Carrom Khela (Carrom Game)

Carrom is an internationally emerging indoor, tabletop game. It is thought to have originated approximately two hundred years ago in the Indian subcontinent. It is one of the most popular indoor games in Bangladesh.

Bangladesh has a national federation for this game called the Bangladesh Carrom Federation. Competitive *Carrom* tournaments are held both locally and nationally in schools, colleges, universities, and club associations. The Bangladesh Carrom Federation participates in various international tournaments as well. Besides being an international sensation, *Carrom* is also intertwined with the daily lives of the people of Bangladesh. It is a popular game to play with family members and at social gatherings. People of all ages enjoy this game because it doesn't require a large space or a lot of players. In fact, this game can only be played with two or four players.

A game played between two players is called a single game, and a game played between two teams, each with two players, is called a double game. The elements needed for playing *Carrom* are a *Carrom* board, *Carrom* men or *gooti*, a striker, a board stand, a chair, boric powder, pocket nets, a light, and a light stand. Although the rules of the International Carrom Federation cite one specific measurement for the size of the *Carrom* board, in Bangladesh, there are actually different sizes of boards used. Below is a complete and detailed description of the gameboard, gameplay, and rules as taken from the International Carrom Federation Rules Book.

Description of the *Carrom* game elements:

1. *Carrom* Board:

    a. **Surface:** The *Carrom* board surface is made of plywood or other wood. This plywood should be flat, smooth, and at least 8 mm thick. It will be square, and the length of the ellipse will be a minimum of 73.50 cm and a maximum of 74 cm. The surface should be so smooth that if a striker weighing fifteen grams hits the wooden frame very hard in the opposite direction, the striker will come and go at least 3.5 times.

    b. **Frame:** The top of the board should be fastened on all four sides with hardwood or rosewood. This wood is synced, meaning it won't burst or bend in the cold or heat. The wooden frame shall not be less than 6.35 cm or more than 7.60 cm wide, and its four corners should be curved. The height of the frame from the top of the board should be between 1.90 cm and 2.54 cm. A small wooden square frame should be attached to the bottom of the board to keep it flat.

c. **Pockets:** There will be four round pockets in the board's four corners. These pockets should be made by cutting the plywood attached to the frame at the corners. The diameter of each pocket is 4.45 cm. The diameter of the pocket can be increased up to 0.15 cm.

d. **Board's Baseline:** On each side of the board parallel to the frame, two 46 cm long straight lines of black color should be drawn on top of the board. The bottom line will be 0.50 cm to 0.75 cm wide, and the distance from the frame should be 10.15 cm to 3.17 cm. A circle of 3.18 cm diameter is drawn on each end of the baselines. Inside each of these circles, there will be a smaller, 2.54 cm diameter red circle. These circles are called "base circles," as each circle is drawn so that it touches the ends of the baseline. Moreover, the distance between the base circle on one side and the base circle on the other side is 1.27 cm.

e. **Board's Angle Drawn Arrow:** Four arrows 0.15 cm wide in black should be drawn along the middle of the pocket at each angle of the *Carrom* board. This arrow passes through the space between the two base circles on both sides and 5.00 cm away from the pocket. The length of each arrow shall not exceed

26.70 cm. At the end of each arrow, there is a semicircle with a diameter of 4.35 cm.

    f. **Center Circle:** There is a circle with a diameter of 3.18 cm at the center of the board. This circle is red, and it is called the center circle.

    g. **Outer Circle:** There is another circle 17.00 cm in diameter from the center of the board. This is called the outer circle. The outer circle can have different designs.

2. **Carrom Men or Pucks:** *Carrom* pucks are circular and made of good quality wood. The diameter of the pucks should not be more than 3.17 cm or less than 3.02 cm, and the pucks should be between 0.70 cm and 0.90 cm thick. The edges of the pucks will be smooth and circular. The weight of each puck shall be at least 5.00 grams but not above 5.50 grams. With respect to *Carrom* men, there should be 9 white men, 9 black men, and 1 red piece, called the Queen. Each piece will have the same shape, size, and weight. If the striker hits them, they must move smoothly on the board's surface.

3. **Striker:** The *Carrom* striker is round and smooth, 4.13 cm in diameter, and weighing no more than fifteen grams. Strikers can be made with any material other than metal.

4. **Board Table or Stand:** The table or stand on which the *Carrom* board will be placed should not be less than 63.00 cm or more than 70 cm in height. After placing the board on the stand, the sides of the board will not be raised or lowered and will not move. The board must be placed steadily on the stand.

5. **Stool or Chair:** The height of the stool or chair on which the player plays *Carrom* must be at least 40.00 cm but not over 50 cm, and the chair must not have arms.

6. **Powder:** High-quality powder needs to be used to play *Carrom* so that the board's surface is smooth and dry. When

using powder from a box, it should be spread evenly over the entire board.

7. **Net:** Nets are used under each pocket of the *Carrom* board so that if pucks fall in the pocket, they can be caught and stored in the net. A net that can hold at least ten pucks needs to be used.

8. **Light:** The bulb's power can be sixty or one hundred watts for convenient lighting of the *Carrom* board. However, arrangements must be made so that the light does not hit players directly in the eye.

Gameplay:

1. **Toss:** The act of "calling the *Carrom* men" or "the toss" establishes the order of play. A referee conceals one black *Carrom* piece in one hand and a white one in the other before each match begins. Participants guess the color of the *Carrom* men that are grasped in each hand. The one who makes an accurate guess wins the toss.

2. **Opening Break:** An opening break is done to initiate the game. The player who does the opening break must play the white *Carrom* men in the game. The opponent must play the black men. The victor of the toss is normally the one to do the first break (and play the white men), however, the toss winner has the option to switch from white to black and forfeit the first break. The toss winner cannot transfer this choice to the other player. If the toss winner decides to switch sides, then they forfeit their turn, and the toss loser has to go first. In this case, their opponent may play any *Carrom* man, black or white, in their favor if they cannot earn any points.

3. **Shooting:** A player is entitled to another shot if a pot (pocket) is successful. This rule is similar to snooker and pool and enables a player to pocket all of their pieces and

cover the Queen at the beginning of the game to prevent the opposition from having a chance to shoot. Any player that pockets the Queen on the entitlement shot must cover it immediately by pocketing one of their *Carrom* men. If the player does not cover the Queen after it has been pocketed, the Queen is placed back in the center of the table. Since the Queen must always be covered, it is forbidden to pot the Queen after the final piece. The International Carrom Federation permits thumbing, also referred to as a "thumbshot," or "thumb hit," which permits the player to shoot with any finger, including the thumb. Also, crossing the diagonal lines on the board by making contact with them is a foul. A player must ensure that their striking hand does not physically or aerially encroach upon or cross the diagonal lines. When players foul, they have to return one *Carrom* man that was previously pocketed. A player will also be penalized if they pocket their striker. Usually, this is a ten-point penalty.

General Rules for the Players:

1. The stroke will be taken only with the striker. A player will bring their own striker and allow the chief referee to examine the striker before the game. During the game, if any puck falls into the red pocket and the striker doesn't jump out of the *Carrom* board while taking the stroke, the player may continue to play using the same striker. After completion of a board, new strikers can be used with the approval of the referee. However, if the striker breaks while taking a stroke, a new striker can be used after the end of that stroke.

2. Changing the position of the *Carrom* board in the middle of the competition isn't allowed. The power to change it rests solely with the referee.

3. The *Carrom* board, table, or *Carrom* board stand can be changed after a game is completed. It will be up to the referee to decide on this.

4. If an application is made to replace a broken puck, the referee will replace it with another and place it in the exact place.

5. The time count will be stopped if an appeal is made to the referee during the game. The game clock will start again once the referee orders play to resume. If a player disobeys the referee's order, points for all of their pieces on the board will be given to the opposing player. If red is on the board at that time, its points will also go to the opposing player.

6. Before taking the first stroke of the board, a player can spread the powder evenly. After play begins, powder cannot be added or removed.

7. Powder cannot be intentionally removed or wiped from the top of the board. Powder cannot be wiped off with a cloth, by hand, by blowing it off, or in any other way. A foul will be declared against the offending player for violating these rules. However, when it is a player's turn, they can remove excess powder from the baseline and base circle with their striker. The referee will make sure that the powder is evenly distributed throughout the game. The referee must be asked to remove any dust or sand that may fall on the board during the game.

8. A stroke will be considered complete if the striker stops moving after hitting a puck or red. After the strike, the player will remove the striker from the board. The referee can help if the striker is asked to be removed.

9. The time clock runs as long as a player continues to drop pucks or red in pockets. This time or countdown clock will continue until their strike is over. But if a player can't drop a puck or red in a pocket in any stroke, then the countdown

clock for the opposing player will begin as soon as the striker has been lifted off the board. Both players can only take the next strike once the opposing player's striker has been removed from the board.

10. The referee will stop the game if a player pockets an opponent's puck. If the umpire or the opposing player does not notice, then the opponent's puck will be assumed to have fallen properly in the pocket.

11. No player may intentionally or otherwise hit, push, or move the *Carrom* board, or a foul will be declared against them. However, as a result of such a movement, if the position of the board's pieces becomes erratic and it is impossible to return it to the previous state, then that player will lose, and all the pucks and red points on the board will be given to the opposing player.

12. If the striker slips out of the baseline or base circle, it will be considered a completed strike whether it touches any pucks or red. However, the strike will only be considered completed if the striker slips and also leaves the base circle.

13. Only during their turn can a player get their points from the referee.

14. A player cannot do anything to distract or interrupt their opponent's focus.

15. The striker must be touching both baselines while taking the stroke. If a player wants to take a stroke from the base circle, they must cover it completely without touching the arrow.

16. During a professional match, the two players will not be able to talk or exchange information with each other in any way. Violation of this rule is punishable by declaring a foul under the provisions of the law. Players can only speak to the spectators during the game with the referee's permission.

17. When it is a player's turn, they cannot hold any metal other than the striker.

18. After the break or the first stroke, the board pieces or the red must not be touched or moved in any way, except by the striker during play. If this happens, the referee will place the displaced puck or red back in its proper place, and a foul will be declared against the offending player as per the provisions of the law.

19. Players can't test their striker's speed on the board by hitting it.

20. A player cannot place their striker on the frame while the board (round) continues. However, they can leave a fallen puck in the pocket or leave their striker near the board.

21. If players from both teams pass three times in a row without actually taking a stroke, the board (round) will be declared abandoned, and the board (round) will have to be played again.

22. There will be a ten-minute break between the second and third boards (rounds).

23. Players can accept defeat at any stage of the competition.

24. If, for some unavoidable reason, the board's pieces become disheveled and impossible to reorganize, then that particular board must be replayed.

25. If the puck breaks due to a strike, the position of the largest of the broken pieces must always be taken as the spot, and for this type of matter, the referee's decision must always be taken as final.

26. If the player's pucks are all over the baseline and the base circle and there is no space to place the striker, then the board must be played again.

115. Shui-Shoota Khela (Threading the Needle Game)

This game is a fun activity among village girls in Bangladesh. It is so popular that it is often included in the annual sports competition at schools and colleges.

To begin, the girls stand in a line at the starting line, and each is given a needle and a piece of thread. A finish line is drawn thirty to fifty feet away, in front of the contestants. There is also a referee present. A flute begins to play, and the competition to insert the thread in the eye of the needle begins. After successfully threading the needle, the contestants must run to the finish line. Whoever crosses the line first wins. Second and third place are also determined in the same way.

There is some risk with this game, as the needles can prick the players' hands and cause bleeding if handled clumsily and hurriedly. However, the excitement to win the game is so great that participants often don't care about the pain and injuries. Some don't even realize they have hurt themselves until later on when the excitement simmers down. Players usually enjoy the game so much that they naturally accept the risks as a part of it.

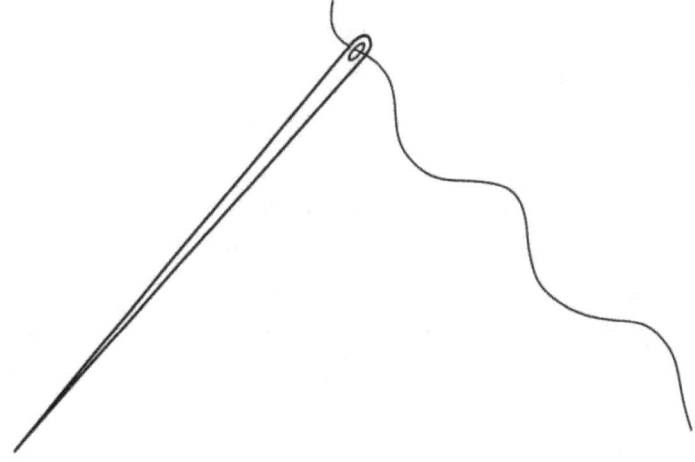

116. Roshi Taana Khela (Tug of War)

Roshi Taana Khela is especially popular among people who do physical labor in the Bogra region of northern Bangladesh. To play this game, a twenty to thirty-foot length of strong rope is required. Players divide themselves into two teams with four or five players on each team. The *mooliya* (team leader) of each team wraps one end of the rope around their waist in a way that won't hurt them. Other team members stand in a line in front of their team leader, holding onto the rope. Both teams try to pull the other team in their direction using all their strength. Sometimes, to increase team spirit, they recite rhymes in unison such as, "Mountains can be moved with team strength."

Before the game begins, a center point is marked on the ground as well as two victory lines two feet on either side of the center point in the direction of each team. A colorful cloth or towel is tied in the middle of the rope and hung so that the judges or spectators can easily see when the cloth crosses one of the victory lines and identify the winning team. A time limit of less than one hour is set for the game. If the cloth tied in the middle crosses one of the victory lines on either side of the center, the team that pulled it across their line gets one point. The team with the most points when time is up wins. In many cases, even after the full time has passed, both parties remain deadlocked in the same position. If both parties' scores are equal, or there is no score, the game goes on to the second phase.

For the second phase, all the players restart at their original positions along the rope. The second phase is very short, usually about five minutes, during which all players try their hardest. If one team can pull the cloth to their side, they win, and the game is over. Otherwise, if the cloth stays in the center for the entire five minutes, there is no winner.

117. Koosti Khela (Wrestling Game)

Koosti Khela is similar to a modern-day wrestling show. *Koosti* (wrestling) is a Persian word. It is still unknown when this word started being used instead of the Bangla *mollo krira* (wrestling).

During the Mughal period (16th-18th centuries), wrestling became more popular in the Indian subcontinent. Emperors Babur, Humayun, Akbar, and many others were all fans of wrestling as well as experts in wrestling themselves. At that time, saints and monks also arranged wrestling lessons for the disciples in their respective arenas. *Honoomaanti, Bhimseni, Jaarashaandhi,* and *Shoorseni* are the four wrestling methods. All of these were formed in the Guru tradition: punching, fist fighting, scratching, throwing, whacking on the head, twisting the legs, breaking the steel chain, breaking the bell (a fruit) while placing it on the chest, and performing various acrobatic feats holding *maalkot* (wood). The *maallaavirs* (wrestlers) rehearsed all of this in their respective arenas. They would also do pushups, sit-ups, barbell lifts, dumbbell curls, and more to build up their bodies.

Wrestlers have been respected and esteemed in the royal court since the Mughal period, and toward the end of the English period, they were still somewhat important. From the beginning of the nineteenth century, the kings and feudal lords continued to employ professional wrestlers to maintain their hobbies and influence. They began to award the winner the Guru's (Master's) title of *"Gooroojbondh"* as well as a cash prize. The spread of this sport among modern-day Bengalis has been impressive, as wrestling has become popular in both upper and middle-class societies alike.

Chapter 2: Animal Shows, Performances, and Festival Games

118. Kobootorer Khela (Pigeon Show)

Kobootorer Khela (Pigeon Show) is very similar to pigeon shows in the US. Those who have domestic pigeons train them to do tricks and engage in different games. These shows are popular in both the towns and villages of Bangladesh. One of the reasons for using pigeons for such shows is because, even if the pigeons are released while performing the show and fly thousands of miles away, they can successfully return to their homes and their owners. Pigeons need to be well-trained to fly before using them in the shows, however.

Among the games the locals play using pigeons, one of the interesting ones is "marrying" pigeons between neighboring pigeon owners. Villagers sometimes arrange a marriage ceremony and marry off unmated pigeons from one neighborhood to another. Young children find this game especially funny and enjoy watching it very much. The female pigeon becomes the bride, and the male becomes the groom. This game is also a nice way of strengthening bonds among the village neighbors.

119. Chaamri Khela (Pond Game)

Chaamri Khela is a game of acting out a particular story. These types of dramatic performances are a source of great entertainment for villagers.

At the beginning of the game, a player acting as the captain of an army uses a stick to mark a court on the ground that represents a pond. His "army" splits into two groups and lines up around the pond. Then, their opponents come and try to clear the area with a stick, and they start fighting.

This fight eventually turns into an excellent stick-fighting game. When the stick game gets going, with its different gestures and rhythms, different types of musical instruments are played to follow along with the rhythm of the stick game. After playing for a while, the two sides raise their sticks toward the sky and make a truce. In a compromise, they split the pond by throwing a towel vertically onto the court. Then, both sides use their sticks to start fishing in the make-believe pond.

To make the fishing scene more real, a group of people pour water on the marked pond shape on the ground, and the players start dipping their hands and feet in the water. Everyone starts competing with each other for attention. While rolling in the mud, actors pretend to catch fish for a while.

But then an accident happens to a player. He says that a catfish's thorn has pricked his hand and starts crying and screaming. Unable to bear the screaming of that person, the others call a doctor. The doctor comes and starts treating the patient with incantations and spells. But it doesn't help, and he starts screaming twice as loud in pain. He starts saying, "Come here! Oh, my dear mother, please come to me! I'm dying from the catfish poison." Hearing him screaming, his mother starts panicking. She comes to her son hastily, stands by him, and starts caring for him. But even her heartiest care can't heal him.

He shouts again and calls for his sister, "Come here! Oh, my sister, please come to me! I'm dying from the catfish poison!" Hearing this, his sister arrives. But she also fails to relieve the pain.

In the end, hearing the screams, a beautiful young woman arrives, stands in front of him, and looks at him with a smile on her face. After that, the words and expressions exchanged through their eyes completely heal the injured man. The story ends there, which romanticizes a couple's connection.

Although both male and female characters are in the story, young boys may also play the female roles. The game is popular in some areas in the Rangpur and Gaibandha districts.

120. Bhallook Naacher Khela (Bear Dancing Show)

Bhallook Naacher Khela is a performance show usually organized during Eid. A group of performers (usually eight to ten) go from house to house to perform their show and ask for money in return. In addition to money, they also accept food and clothing as payment. People of all ages enjoy this show.

The performers are usually older men; one plays the master of the bears, and the others play the bears. The bear master has a stick and a small kettle drum known locally as *doogdoogy*. He also wears an enormous turban on his head. The others playing bears wear bearskin, loincloths, and masks made of gourd shells. Then, they dance around and sing songs in nasal tunes.

121. Ghoori Ooraano (Kite Flying)

Kite flying is very popular in Bangladesh, just like in other parts of Asia. This game was first introduced in China, where the oldest record of a kite is from over 2,000 years ago. From there, it gradually gained popularity in Japan, Korea, Singapore, Thailand, and India. In Hamamatsu, Japan, a very lavish ceremony is conducted on the first day of the Kite Festival, and that day is also a public holiday. In Tibet, large kites in the shape of cages are known to transport people to inaccessible places.

In Bangladesh, the game is just as popular. Towards the end of the year, as soon as the weather turns dry and windy, people start flying kites in both large towns and small villages alike. People in villages fly kites in open fields, and the townspeople do so from the roofs or terraces of tall buildings. During the winter and spring months, kites fill the sky creating an eye-catching scene of bold colors like white, black, red, and blue. The most popular kites are the "airplane kites," "drum kites," and "chang kites."

There are some rhymes that village people like to recite while watching kites fly that reflect local kite-flying myths. Those rhymes say that the kites need to be brought down, and they shouldn't be allowed to fly so high. Otherwise, they will puncture the sky, and rainwater will come down along the kite string and flood the whole world!

At the end of the twentieth century, kite flying had become quite popular amongst children and adults alike. It was often played competitively, and pitchers, radios, and cups were given as prizes. There was even a committee to manage the competitions, which sometimes lasted from seven to fifteen days.

The game played at the competitions is known as "Twisting of the Kites," and an entry fee is collected from participants. Spectators hear beating drums or blowing trumpets in the market and know that a kite-flying game is about to begin in a nearby park or playground. Gamblers and vendors with sweets, earthen dolls, and more suddenly appear in the vicinity of the area to service the crowd.

The teams or individuals who typically participate in the kite-twisting games are the youth and young adults of the village. To prepare for the competition, participants create a mixture of egg yolk, rice liquid, glass powder, sand, and cow dung and place it along the string of their kite. After it dries, this sharpens the string. The main goal of this game is to cut the strings of all the other kites while playing the game. When a kite is cut, it can fall one to two kilometers, or more, away. Children and teenagers like to run after the fallen kites, as the one who recovers the kite gets to keep it. The chase to find the fallen kites is also quite fun. There is also a wonderful song about kite flying which goes, "I tied the string to the kite and let it go, go! Fly in the wind now, go!"

The role of West Bengal in India was invaluable in introducing the game of kites as a competition. West Bengal kite players formed the West Bengal Kite Association in 1954. Of course, there were many kite clubs in India even before that, such as the Kite Flying Federation of India, but the West Bengal Kite Association brought new ideas to the activity.

122. Choonga Khela (Firecracker Game)

This game used to be played mainly in the Chittagong region on the eve of *Shob-e-Borat*. *Shob-e-Borat* or Borat Night is a significant festival for Muslims, celebrated on the fifteenth night of *Shaa'baan*, the eighth month of the Islamic calendar (usually in February or March). This sacred night starts at sunset on the fifteenth day of *Shaa'baan* and ends at dawn on the sixteenth day of *Shaa'baan*.

The game started around sunset and continued until midnight. People filled up bamboo funnels (called *choonga*) with gunpowder and broken pieces of clay pots to make homemade firecrackers and then formed teams to shoot the firecrackers at each other. If they could hit the opponents successfully, it was deemed a win for their team. These homemade firecrackers were not safe at all and often caused burn injuries. Despite the risk, this game was quite popular and spectacular, with sparks and flashes of fire coupled with deafening sounds amid cheers from spectators.

However, this expensive and dangerous game is now almost extinct. Nowadays, it has become more of a fireworks show, like Fourth of July displays in the US, than a competition of hitting opponents with dangerous materials. Also, people buy safe firecrackers from stores now rather than making dangerous homemade ones.

123. Dhopbaari Khela (Field Hockey Game)

Dhopbaari is a game similar to field hockey that is played mainly on the Bengali New Year (April 14). The main purpose of this game is to say goodbye to the old year and embrace the new one with joy and fun. The game is played primarily in the Tangail and Rangpur districts. The game is called *Vyattadaandi* in the Rangpur district.

The equipment for the game consists of a ball (*dhop* or *vyatta*) and sticks (*baari* or *daandi*), hence the origin of the game names. Medium-sized bamboo with roots is selected to make the equipment. First, the bamboo part is cut from the root and sharpened to turn it into a tool that looks much like a hockey stick. Then, the leftover root is given the shape of a ball (see image). In the Tangail district, instead of the bamboo root, a rope is tied to a piece of wood to give it a round shape. The stick is prepared similarly in both places.

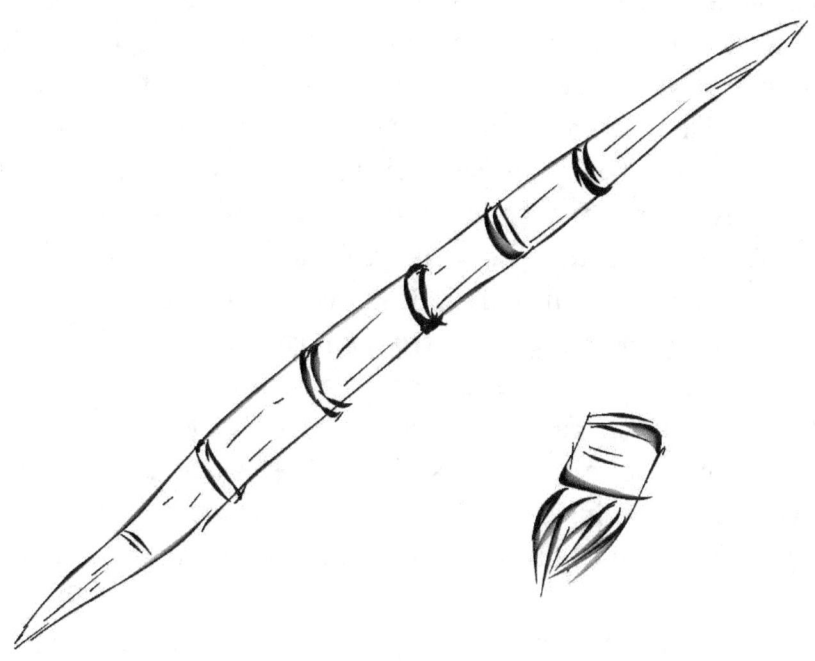

A wide, open area is selected as the playing field, and a rectangle-shaped boundary with a line dividing the rectangle in half are marked. The ball is placed in the center of the middle line to start the game. Two teams play this game, and one is chosen through a toss to go first (Team A). Team A starts to strike the ball with the sticks, trying to put it through a goalpost in Team B's court. Team B's players defend the attack by striking the ball with sticks and moving it back towards Team A's goalpost. When a team can strike the ball into the opponent's goalpost, they get a point. The game goes on like this for a specified amount of time, and the team that scores the most points wins.

124. Laathi Khela (Stick Game)

Laathi Khela (Stick Game) is a traditional Bengali martial art—a kind of theatrical stick fighting practiced throughout Bangladesh. It is usually played on religious or special occasions as it is a game in which a large number of people can participate together, either as players or spectators. Special musicians are hired for these games, and they make music that has significance while the game is going on. The sound of drums can be heard from far away, and one can tell from the music which kind of stick game is being played.

A stick game can go on for several days at a time. During this time, *laathiyal* (stick players) congregate in groups in the main houses of the village, where there are designated areas for playing sticks, and also in the houses where nice rewards or gifts can be obtained for playing sticks. Gifts are given in the form of cash, rice, and other things. A big food festival is organized at the end of the stick game.

Although the stick games last just a few days, the preparations for them usually take much longer. On rainy, autumn nights, the masters organize training sessions for stick players. Also, there is a rush to make sticks, *shaarkaari, baanri*, shields, and other equipment needed for the game. Not only the *laathiyal* but also many non-players help in preparing the bamboo, cane, and other materials needed for the stick-playing equipment.

Through the stick game, the *laathiyal* depict the joys and sorrows of rural life, romance, and various historical stories. Occasionally there are shows of various types of magic, betting, and even thrilling events during the game.

In addition to sticks, many other tools are needed for stick playing. There are also special drums and musical instruments for players. The main materials are briefly described below:

1. Sticks: Three types of sticks are required for playing, but the size, use, and technique for making them are different.

a. Slender sticks or *nori*: These sticks are made with hard bash slices and are three feet long. This type of stick is made by cutting a big bamboo into four to six slices and specially thrashing the slices with a sharp chopper. Before the game, 100-250 such sticks must be made and collected.

b. Medium-size sticks: The length of this stick is four to five feet. The stick is made from the thin part of bamboo tips. Before the start of the game, 40-55 medium-size sticks must be made.

c. Large sticks: The *laathiyal* make the big sticks all by themselves. They cut the right bamboo and process it by heating it with fire and oil. The bamboo knots are cut in a particular manner. The sticks are coated with oil, butter, and ghee in a way that will help them last for fifty to one hundred years. Some sticks may have been passed down in the family through the generations. In creating and customizing their sticks, the *laathiyal* can better demonstrate their stick-wielding skills during the game. They can move the stick so fast that the stick cannot be seen. Even if ten or twelve people try hitting them, their opponents' sticks will not hit the body of the *laathiyal*.

2. *Shaarkaari*: *Shaarkaari* is a type of war weapon made of bamboo used by the *laathiyal* to capture the alluvial lands. A hard, strong, large bamboo is cut thirty to forty feet long and divided into four slices, each made into a *shaarkaari*. They are made sharp and pointy, and, in many cases, sharp edges of iron or steel are added to the far end. With this, a skilled *shorkibaj* (a person who wields a *shaarkaari*) can smash the body of a human or even a large wild animal. Before starting the game, ten to twelve *shaarkaari* are made and deposited.

3. *Baanri*: A *baanri* is a special kind of thin stick. Thick bamboo has to be sliced into pieces four to five feet long. Two are attached to two wooden balls, making it look like a club. *Baanri* are needed only in certain types of games. However, special-trained *laathiyal* are required for twirling the *baanri* in a specific way. They twist and twirl the *baanri* so fast that it can't be seen. During *baanri* twirling, even if one hits the *laathiyal*, it doesn't harm his body. Eight to ten pairs of *baanri* have to be prepared before the start of the game.

4. Shield: Different-sized shields are used in stick games to defend the opponent's attack. The shield is made of cane. To strengthen the shield, it has to be wrapped with matte leather. A soft leather belt is fastened to hold the shield tightly and comfortably.

How to Start Playing Sticks:

Laathiyal must first calculate the payment they can receive for playing at a certain house by discussing what kind of gift or money can be offered.

Then, they arrive at the house where the game of sticks will be played, carrying the drums and stick-playing equipment. The *laathiyal* prepare to start the game with the permission of the landlord. The musicians are seated in places with shade or under a canopy and start playing before the game begins. Hearing the sound of the drums, the people know which house is playing stick, and they start coming in lines to watch the game.

The players gather in the field with their sticks and other tools before the game starts and dance to the beat of the instruments. Special players start circling the field and sometimes dance in two groups. Then, another special game is arranged to show a unique story. The *laathiyal* present a story of the laughter and tears of rural life or a historical event through the stick games.

Rules of Gameplay:

The rules for playing thin sticks or medium sticks are the same. However, different types of games are played with these two types of sticks. The players enter the field in pairs and then split into two groups. When an individual player competes against a team, two to four players go up against the individual. To start the game, the players participate in a variety of dances in a circular manner. During a cross dance, one side shows sharp gestures toward the other. Then, they attack each other. If the attack is not successfully defended, the sticks will hit different parts of the body.

When a team of more than one player competes against more than one player from the other team, the game ends with a double contest. That is, two players from each team fight against each other. The loser either raises their hand and surrenders or leaves the field standing.

125. Shorki Khela (Acting out a Historical Story)

Shorki Khela is a traditional game where a historical story of great significance to the Muslims is performed. The players act as the *laathiyal* (soldiers armed with sticks) and act out the battle of Yazid's forces versus the forces of Hazrat Hassan, the son of Hazrat Ali (RA), in the desert of Karbala. These are all prominent Muslim figures, and the Battle of Karbala is one of the most significant wars in Islamic history.

The fighting teams each have at least five players. The team leader stands in the middle of the team, equipped with a *shorki* (a thin stick) in one hand and a shield in the other. On either side of the leader are two comrades with similar weapons. On the ends are two or more warriors with medium-sized sticks.

The players of both teams enter the field together. To begin, they perform circular dances of various poses, moving around the field together. Then, they perform a cross dance. During the cross dance, the players of one team shout aggressively at the opposing team and make gestures. At the end of the dance, they shout and separate into their two teams, starting war preparations.

Before the conflict begins, both sides shout at each other and call for war. People make strange noises by clapping their hands while giving a war roar. Yazid's army shouts and asks for the identity of the other team by saying a rhyme:

> *Kon deshe shohor tomaar?* (In which city do you live?)
>
> *Kon shohore ghor?* (In which city is your home?)
>
> *Keba tomaar maatapeetaa? Kiba porichoy? Re re re...* (Who is your father? What is your identity? Rah, rah, rah...)

Hearing the roar, Hassan's (RA's) team leader shouts in the same manner but even louder. Hassan's team leader responds to Yazid's war cries:

> *Mokkaat baari aamar, Modinaat ghor.* (My house is in Makkah, Madina is my home.)

Baabaar naamti Aali Shah. Naana poigombor, re re re... (My father's name is Ali Shah. The prophet is my great grandfather, rah, rah, rah...)

Again, Yazid's team leader shouts in the same manner as before:
Mokkaat baari tomaar, Modinaat ghor. (Your house is in Makkah. Madina is your home.)
Paani khaich kon nodir? (Which river water do you drink?)
Doodh khaai kaar? Re re re... (Whose milk did you drink? Rah, rah, rah...)

Hassan's party again shouts:
Mokkaat baari aamar, Modinaat ghor. (My house is in Makkah. Madina is my home.)
Paani khaaichi Foorot nodir. (I drink water from the Furat River.)
Doodh khaaichi maa Faatimaar. Re re re... (I drank my mother Fatima's milk. Rah, rah, rah...)

With this war cry, Hassan's team jumps on Yazid's team, and a fierce battle begins. The play area transforms into the battlefield of Karbala with counterattacks and battle cries. The audience waits anxiously to see which party wins and loses. In the real battle of Karbala, Hassan's forces were defeated by Yazid's. The most significant part of the re-enactment is the fight between the two team leaders. One attacks the other and shouts so that it seems one will kill the other. The war cries, battle dances, roleplay, acting, and culturally significant story make the *Shorki* game really popular with both players and audiences alike.

126. Hoo Koot Koot/Chaalachaali Khela (Test of Strength and Balance)

Hoo koot koot/Chaalachaali Khela is a game of strength and balance. The game used to be very popular in the Rangpur and Patuakhali districts, however, the game is extinct now.

This game was usually played in the villages on the holy days of *Eid-ul-Fitr* and *Eid-ul-Azhar*, to bring the joy of Eid to life. The youth tested their strength and courage through this game. Sometimes, the game would lead to quarrels and fights. For this game, a small area of ground was thoroughly cleaned and chopped up with a spade. People would break up all the clods of soil, dust the area, and then pour water on it until it was completely slippery and muddy. It would be made so slippery that it would be difficult to stand there and maintain balance. However, young people would challenge each other to stand there and, on top of that, carry another person on their shoulders. Whoever managed to succeed in this cumbersome challenge was deemed worthy of admiration and known in the village as the *Polayon* (acrobat).

127. Hoomghooti Khela (Carrying the Pitcher Game)

Hoomghooti Khela is one of the most popular games in the Mymensingh district, and it is mainly played in the Muktagachha and Fulbaria sub-districts. However, it isn't played anywhere else in Bangladesh. This game is played as a competition among neighboring villages during a special occasion each year. The competitive theme reflects the characteristics of feudal society in Bangladesh. Before hosting the game, the date and time of the game are announced by beating drums in the *haat baazaar* (local market) of the participating villages. On that date and time, people come to see the game, even from far away.

The main item needed for this game is a brass pitcher. The mouth of this brass pitcher is cut off, and the pitcher is filled with sugar. Then the opening of the pitcher is welded shut. The pitcher now looks more like a big ball and weighs over twenty kilograms (see image). In this form, it is called a *ghooti*, and it makes a humming sound while moving. It is from this "humming" sound that the name of the game became *Hoomghooti*.

The village that will initiate the game prepares the *ghooti*. When the *ghooti* is prepared, a strong man from that village grabs it and becomes the village's main representative. All the people from his village accompany and guard him while he starts to carry the *ghooti* toward the neighboring village. People from the neighboring village come out to participate in the game. They aim to block this party and try to take away the *ghooti*. But that doesn't come easy if the hosting village's defensive players are strong. But if players from the neighboring village can snatch the *ghooti* away, they will try to bring it to the next village. This way, the *ghooti* gets transferred to field after field, village after village, and may even travel up to thirty or forty miles.

A strange rule of this game is that, while carrying the *ghooti,* if there is any obstruction along the way, like trees or even a house, it will be immediately cut down or removed from the path, and no one can say anything about it. Rather, the people who have their property demolished accept the loss. A game of *Hoomghooti* can go on like this for two to four days. If any team manages to hide the *ghooti* from the players of another village, their village wins the game and is rewarded.

128. Hoo-Hoo Paata Khela (The Leaf Game)

Hoo-Hoo Paata Khela is an old game involving magic that is no longer played at this time. The game only exists by name in the Barisal region. This game requires no physical exertion or strength but rather the manifestation of hypnotic energy. Due to the direct influence of magic, the game likely originates back to ancient times.

This game does not have a specific formal occasion or time that it is played. The game can be played in any open area, such as the backyard of a home, a street corner, a garden, a field, etc. A person of the Libra sign is chosen as the *paata* (leaf). After the mantra is recited, this person is blown on and their hand starts shaking. Two wise persons (people who have a vast knowledge of mantra and magic) then recite mantras from two sides, some distance away, and the *paata* runs in the direction where the mantra's power is stronger. It has been said that during the game, a certain wise person was once reciting a mantra from far away, and the *paata* left the other two wise men, crossing fields and villages, to appear before that person. Sometimes, the *paata* gets cuts and wounds from sprinting but doesn't feel anything as they are under magical influence and not fully aware of what is happening around them.

Another important participant in this game is the *dhooli*, as the game is incomplete without the special music of the *dhooli's* drums. This is a major part of the game's attraction. The *dhooli* in this game is usually not a professional, as opposed to other games, but merely someone who plays drums as a hobby. This person is skilled and experienced, but they only play drums for certain purposes as their drums are *montropoota* (enchanted with mantras).

According to local folklore, as far as the special rhythmic sound of the drums can reach, people under the Libra sign in the immediate area get enchanted and voluntarily appear in the playing area; they don't necessarily have to be chosen. They then become the *paata*. Next, the wise men gather around to show off their own magic and sorcery. Magicians influence the *paata* by cutting spots on the ground, either openly or secretly, or by moving their hands. The wise man who manages to pull and hold the *paata* to them has more power and skill, and thus, the victory becomes theirs. The drums keep beating from the beginning to the last moment of the game.

Curious and excited onlookers crowd around to see and enjoy the magic along with the music from the drums. The winner gets a reward, and the *dhooli* receives a payment.

Works Cited

"Bangladesh Carrom Federation," *Wikipedia*,
en.wikipedia.org/wiki/Bangladesh_Carrom_Federation
Accessed 1 October 2024.

"Carrom," *Banglapedia*, en.banglapedia.org/index.php/Carrom
Accessed 1 October 2024.

"Roomaal Chor," *The Daily Star,* www.thedailystar.net/playtime-39841. Accessed 1 October 2024.

"Sixteen Soldiers," *Wikipedia*,
en.wikipedia.org/wiki/Sixteen_Soldiers
Accessed 1 October 2024.

About the Author

Raju Mahajan was born and raised in Bangladesh. From childhood, he was involved in many co-curricular activities like creative writing, debate, public speaking, poetry recitation, and theatre. After obtaining his undergrad degree, he worked as an FM radio producer from 2008 to 2011.

Raju published his first fiction work in 2010 at the Ekushey Book Fair, the largest and most prestigious book fair in Bangladesh. Since then, he has continued to write and publish fiction, non-fiction, and self-help materials in both the English and Bengali languages. The main theme of his fiction books is usually social critique. His non-fiction books, on the other hand, are highly influenced by tradition, folklore, and history.

Raju is an immigration attorney by profession and is admitted to the Supreme Court of the United States. He is also actively involved in multiple for-profit and non-profit initiatives. He ran for public office and narrowly lost.

In his personal life, Raju thinks that his superpower is persistence. He is a very extroverted people person, and his favorite vacation spot is in the mountains. Raju is father to a toddler daughter, and his world moves around her. For those who would like to contact him, his email address is raju@rajulaw.com.

More by Raju Mahajan

A unique examination of supercharacters in the West and the East, Neelkamal: The Bengali Batman addresses key differences and similarities between America's Batman and Bangladesh's Neelkamal to highlight civilization's view of its heroes. The first of its kind, this analysis celebrates the diversity of societal traditions and invites the reader on a journey toward greater cultural understanding for future cooperation between societies.

Scan the QR code below to purchase the book.